First Aid for Dogs

First published in Australia in 2005 by
New Holland Publishers (Australia) Pty Ltd
Sydney • Auckland • London • Cape Town

1/66 Gibbes Street Chatswood NSW 2067 Australia
218 Lake Road Northcote Auckland New Zealand
86 Edgware Road London W2 2EA United Kingdom
80 McKenzie Street Cape Town 8001 South Africa

Reprinted in 2008
Copyright © 2005 in text: Justin Wimpole
Copyright © 2005 in images: Gregory Lamont
Copyright © 2005 New Holland Publishers (Australia) Pty Ltd

National Library of Australia Cataloguing-in-Publication Data:

Wimpole, Justin.
            First aid for dogs.

            Includes index.
            ISBN 9781741102826

            1. Dogs - Wounds and injuries - Treatment. 2. Dogs - Diseases - Treatment.
            3. First aid for animals - Handbooks, manuals, etc. I. Title.

            636.7089710262

Publisher: Fiona Schultz
Managing Editor: Martin Ford
Production Controller: Linda Bottari
Project Editor: Michael McGrath
Designer: Gregory A Lamont
Printer: McPherson's Printing Group, Victoria
Cover Image: Getty Images

First Aid for Dogs

By Dr Justin Wimpole — BVSc (hons)

NEW
HOLLAND

Acknowledgments

Many people have helped me through my training to become a veterinarian and deserve recognition and thanks. My parents, Denis and Helena, have always been supportive of all of my pursuits throughout my schooling in Melbourne and university in Sydney. My brother has been a great mate and very encouraging.

My special thanks go to my partner, Dr Kate Patterson, who has been my companion through both the relaxing and the challenging times. Her family: Roger, Janice and Lisa has always been open and welcoming, for which I am most appreciative. My gratitude goes to my diverse group of friends, who have been so much fun and have given me support and guidance.

I thank my dedicated and dynamic colleagues in the Veterinary profession, who continue to inspire me, especially my colleges at the Veterinary Specialist Centre and the Animal Critical Care and Emergency Service in North Ryde. I have been privileged to work with you and share your expertise. I extend a special thanks to my mentors: Professor Trevor Heath, Professor David Fraser and Professor Klaus Beyenbach who ensured my professional development.

Thanks to Fiona Schultz and the staff at New Holland, for their support and encouragement, and to my agents Clare Calvet and Xavier Waterkeyn of Flying Pigs. Thanks in particular to Xavier, my friendly, experienced mentor and a writer himself. He provided vital advice and assistance in writing this, my first book.

Finally I would like to thank my patients. You are all very different and very special. You teach me new things every day.

Contents

Introduction

Dogs are a very special part of our lives. They provide unconditional love and companionship and are integral parts of our families. Dogs become our family and we become their pack. As well as providing friendship dogs serve their owners in more tangible ways. There are countless stories of dogs rescuing their owners from attackers or alerting their families to danger. Many people rely on their dogs for work: think of the contribution dogs make to the police, to the military and the vital role of guard dogs. The Beagle's accurate sense of smell and obsession for food makes them a valuable addition to our quarantine service. Guide dogs provide life changing help to their visually impaired owners while assistance and companion dogs provide a variety of valuable services to their disabled owners.

Although dogs are so helpful and important to our lives, they rely on people to care for them. Due to their importance to us and their dependence on us we want to look after them. When our dogs are sick or injured we want to do all that we can to help them. Unfortunately, there are many hazards to our faithful companions. We can easily find ourselves in situations where they need our help, but we may feel helpless and ill prepared to be of any assistance.

As dogs have become a more and more important part of our society, the range of available veterinary services has improved. There are 24-hour emergency centres in most capital cities and in some regional centres too. Most areas have veterinarians who provide after-hours service on an as-needed call-out basis. In most instances the best thing that can be done for your sick or injured dog is to seek prompt veterinary attention. This allows professional assessment and access to diagnostic testing and timely treatment.

Unfortunately not all owners have access to veterinary attention at all times. This book provides some basic information to dog owners and carers to better equip them to help their dog in an emergency. It by no means aims to replace or delay veterinary assistance. Treating it as such is dangerous. You should only intervene when it is imperative that something is done immediately, when you have no access to veterinary attention or the closest veterinary hospital is far away. Sometimes an owner can save their dog's life by giving appropriate first aid.

When I provide veterinary attention to animals, I always attempt to apply the philosophy of 'do no harm'. The information in this book is presented with that principle in mind. Unfortunately, when owners or even veterinarians try to help a sick or injured dog, there is the potential to cause more harm. This is obviously not intentional. It is imperative that first aid given to a sick or injured dog helps the dog's situation rather than hinders it.

By reading this book to better equip yourself for emergencies involving your dog you are showing a real commitment to your companion. Hopefully you will never have to use the information presented in this book, but should the need arise you will be better equipped to deal with the situation.

Disclaimer

This book was written to offer dog owners and lovers first aid advice when dealing with emergencies involving dogs. It was written using veterinary knowledge and experience, but should never be used as a substitute for professional assessment, advice or care. In some instances providing first aid has the potential to cause harm to the patient and the person providing it. It is the responsibility of the reader to consider these risks when deciding on a course of action in any particular situation. Readers should be aware that, even with the benefit of a veterinary hospital setting, the outcome of emergency situations can be undesirable including permanent injury or loss of life. Results can be expected to be even less successful in the field situation. The illustrations have been included as a guide and are not intended to be complete, step-by-step instructions.

The author and publisher cannot be held responsible for any loss or personal injury caused by the application of any advice provided in this book.

If in doubt, please contact your nearest veterinary hospital immediately.

For 'Magic' Burnley 3rd August 2000 to 6th September 2004.
Magic was an Australian show champion and a champion in the eyes of all that knew her.
She lived life to the full and tried her best right until the end, as did her family.
She is gone but not forgotten.

Being Prepared

The most important aspect in being prepared for an emergency involving your dog is to have a good ongoing relationship with your veterinarian. You can easily achieve this by attending to your dog's routine preventative medicine requirements. This involves having your dog vaccinated and examined regularly. Regular visits allow you to obtain advice on flea control, intestinal worm and heartworm prevention, diet, training and other aspects of caring for your dog. Seeing your veterinarian regularly will also allow your veterinarian to identify and manage your dog's individual issues and be aware of them in case of an emergency.

Become familiar with your local veterinary surgery opening hours. Talk to your veterinarian about provisions for after hours emergencies. Some veterinarians provide their own emergency service on an as-needed call-out basis. Where this type of service is provided some clinics will have live-in staff. Other clinics will divert their emergencies to another close by clinic. Sometimes a group of clinics will share the after-hours service on a roster. On some nights or weekends it will be your clinic, while others it will be another nearby clinic. Some clinics will send their after hours emergencies to a dedicated emergency centre. Often, when a veterinary clinic has a critical patient that requires 24 hour care, they may elect to send them to such a service for ongoing monitoring and treatment overnight.

When you call your regular veterinary surgery's number after hours you may speak to someone directly. There will more likely be clear recorded instructions, perhaps providing the number of a pager or another hospital where you may take your animal. To be best prepared for an emergency however, it is important to know what arrangements your particular veterinary surgery has. After-hours services of all types are usually significantly more expensive than those during regular surgery hours. So if you think that your dog is unwell during normal surgery hours it is much more economical (and much less stressful) to see your veterinarian during normal surgery hours rather than some stranger after hours when your dog's condition may have progressed. Expedient assessment and treatment is also obviously better for your dog.

There is a section called Emergency Contacts on page 111, where you can record all this information as well as other important details and phone numbers.

Knowing your veterinarian's regular surgery hours: what type of after-hours service is provided and where you should go in an after-hours emergency, is very important.

Unfortunately there is no organised animal ambulance service that is available at all times. One common obstacle that owners have in an emergency is transport. If you do not have a car then knowing what type of emergency service is available is especially important. Emergency centres may be much further from your house than your regular veterinary clinic is. Some veterinarians provide a house call service, however, this is not always available after hours. If you do not have access to a car or an ambulatory veterinary service you will have to arrange alternative transport. There are several pet transport services available in metropolitan areas. Unfortunately many of these do not operate after hours. Some taxi companies will transport pets, especially small dogs. Exactly which company will do this is something that you will have to investigate in your area. In an emergency you should specify to the taxi company that you wish to transport a sick animal so that they can send a willing driver. Taxis are obliged to transport seeing guide dogs and assistance dogs. Often owners have to rely on neighbours and friends to provide transport for them and their dogs in an emergency situation if they do not have their own transport.

This book will provide some basic advice on how to help your dog while they are sick or injured. However, it is very beneficial to get to know you dog as well as you can and be as aware as possible of what is normal for them when they are well.

I recommend that you:

- Monitor your dog's water intake and appetite and note any changes in either or both.
- Note their urination. Pay attention to colour, volume, frequency, any straining, the presence of blood and any inability to urinate.
- Note their defecation. Take note of consistency, colour, volume, frequency, any straining and the presence of blood or mucous.

Owners who learn to perform a basic physical examination on their dog are better prepared to help them if they become sick. The more your veterinarian knows about your animal's condition, the better equipped they are to help you. This is especially true if they need to give you advice over the phone.

Gum colour

Your dog's gum colour is something that you can easily check. Simply lift your dog's upper lip or gently pull down on the lower lip and observe the colour of the gums or the inner lip. The normal gum colour of a dog is a healthy pink.

There is some normal variation in this because some dogs will have more black pigment on the lips and gums. Also dogs with short muzzles such as Bulldogs, Shih Tzus and Pekingese tend to have a slightly more intensely pink colour than dogs with longer muzzles, such as German Shepherds or Golden Retrievers.

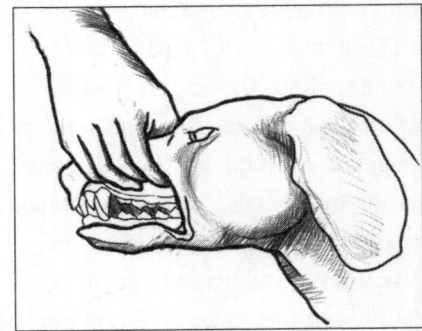

Examining a dog with normal gum colour.

Pale pink or white gums may indicate anaemia (low red blood cell counts), pain or shock. Yellow or jaundiced gums may indicate liver problems, blockage of bile flow or excessive breakdown of red blood cells. Either way, pale to whitish or yellowish gums usually indicate severe illness. Brownish or greyish coloured gums may also indicate ill health.

Some conditions will make the gums a brick red colour. Poor blood oxygen levels can cause the gums to have a bluish tinge (note that the Chow Chow and Shar Pei naturally have a bluish to blackish tinge to the tongue and mouth). Bruising to the gums can indicate a problem with blood clotting.

Heart rate

Another aspect of your dog's health that you can monitor is their heart rate. The easiest way for an owner to do this without a stethoscope is to feel for the heartbeat on the chest wall. You can feel this best on the left hand side of the chest just behind the left elbow. You can feel for this either while they are standing or lying on their side.

An easy way for you to do this is to count the number of beats in 15 seconds and multiply this by four to find the number of beats per minute. The normal resting heart rate of a dog is about 80–120 beats per minute. This should be measured when your dog is calm and resting. Larger dogs tend to have a slower heart rate while you can expect smaller dogs to have a faster heart rate. Some fit dogs will have a heart

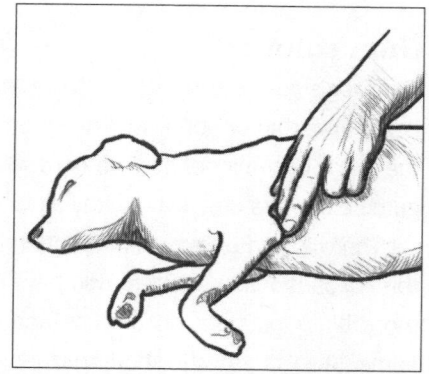

Feeling a dog's chest for a heartbeat.

rate below this range and this may be normal for them. If your dog is over-weight it can be difficult to feel their heartbeat. You can also use a stetho-scope at this point to measure the heart rate if you have one. Many things can cause your dog's heart rate to become elevated, including exercise, excitement or a fright. Illness can also affect a dog's heart rate.

Pulse rate

The pulse rate is usually but not always the same as the heart rate. The best way to measure your dog's pulse rate is to measure the femoral pulse. This is located on the inner surface of the thigh. This is a little more difficult to locate than the heartbeat and may require more practice. You can most easily find this when your dog is upright by standing behind them, reaching in front of their thigh and gently feeling for the pulse high up on the inner surface of their thigh. Using your index and middle fingers, feel for a groove running down the leg in the middle of the inner thigh

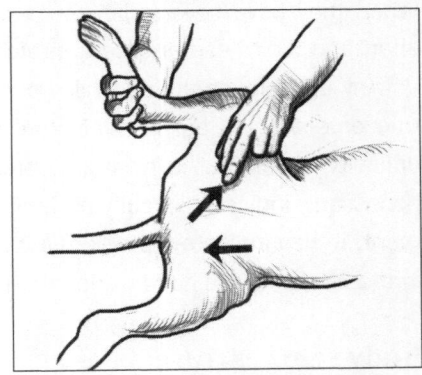
Feeling for the femoral pulse.

where the large blood vessels run. You can also feel for this when they are lying on their side. Finding your dog's pulse can also be difficult if your dog is overweight.

It can be difficult for owners to judge the quality of the pulse. However, if you become familiar with what the pulse is like when your dog is well, you are more likely to be able to describe it when they are unwell. For example it can be weak, normal or bounding.

Breathing

Your dog's rate of breathing and the effort that they need put in to breathing also tells you something about your dog's health. At rest your dog's breathing rate should be around 8–32 breaths per minute however many factors will influence this. Your dog should breathe with minimal effort with only the chest wall moving for the most part. Normally they will breathe through their nose with their mouth closed. When dogs are having difficulty breathing the rate will increase and the chest movements become exaggerated. They may also start to pant uncontrollably. When a dog becomes more distressed, they start breathing with their belly as well as their chest. If the problem is an upper airway obstruction their breathing may also be noisy. Dogs that have difficulty breathing may be restless, reluctant to lie down and unable to sleep. When they have severe difficulty breathing they stand with their forelimbs apart and their head and neck stretched out.

Any difficulty breathing while your dog is completely at rest represents a true emergency. Bear in mind that it is easy to underestimate how much difficulty an animal is having to breathe. Note panting in itself does not necessarily indicate difficulty breathing if it is due to heat, exercise or excitement. It may indicate a problem if it is occurring more regularly than normal in the absence of a good explanation such as after exercise or on a hot day.

Body temperature

Changes in body temperature indicate hypothermia, overheating or fever. The normal body temperature of a dog is warmer than that of a human. So a dog will usually feel warm to touch. This is normal, however this can often be mistaken for a fever. A dog's temperature is most accurately measured rectally. You can do this using either a glass or a digital thermometer. You should shake down glass thermometers before use. The tips of either type of thermometer should be lubricated, preferably with a water-based, lubricant jelly such as KY®. You then insert the thermometer directly into the anus 1–2cm. Then gently angle it to one side so that the tip of the thermometer is up against the rectal wall. A common mistake is to leave the tip of the thermometer in the centre of the rectum, often within a fecal ball. This provides an inaccurate reading because it is measuring the temperature of the feces rather than the core body temperature. Hold onto the thermometer while taking the reading so that it does not inadvertently become lost in your dog's rectum.

Glass analogue thermometers need to be shaken down before use and left in place for around two minutes before you can read them. When using glass thermometers be careful not to break them while they are in your dog's rectum, especially if your dog is very boisterous or if they do not like having their temperature taken. Digital thermometers are generally much quicker and usually beep once they have finished measuring. The normal temperature of a dog is around 37.5°–39.5°C. Many factors influence your dog's body temperature including the temperature of the room, the weather and any activity your dog has been doing. You should take these factors into consideration when measuring body temperature. If the temperature is only just outside the normal range, consider repeating the measurement say after an hour or two to verify that a problem exists.

Know you dog's normal gum colour, heart and pulse rates, breathing patterns and temperature. Practice observing and measuring these things. It is your best chance of detecting a problem if they become unwell.

All dogs are individuals and vary slightly. If you have more than one dog, you need to practice taking measurements on each of them and become familiar with what is normal for each individual.

The First Aid Kit for Your Dog

A canine first aid kit need only contain some very basic supplies for an emergency. One of the most important items in this kit should be your veterinarian's name and contact details. It should also include details of surgery hours and after-hours arrangements. You should also have the details of at least one veterinary emergency centre near you that is open after hours. You should also have the number for the council ranger. During office hours, you can usually contact the ranger through the appropriate council's main line. Some larger councils will have a 24-hour emergency service and the ranger can be contacted through an after-hours number. However other councils only have a ranger service during normal business hours. You should also have the number of the Poisons Information Centre and other important phone numbers, which can be recorded in Emergency Contacts section provided on page 111 at the back of this book.

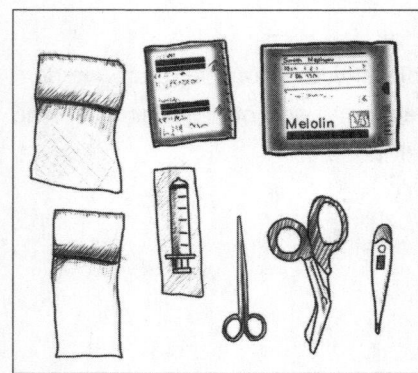

Clockwise from top left: conforming gauze, non-adherent dressings, scissors, digital thermometer, syringe, adhesive bandage.

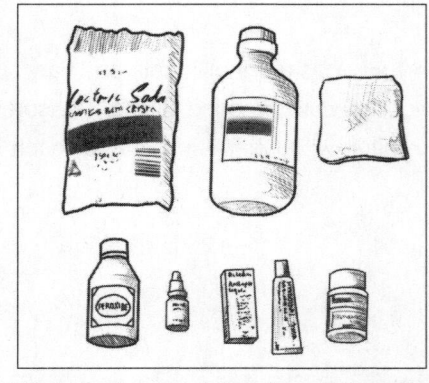

Clockwise from top left: soda crystals, saline solution, gauze swab, 3% hydrogen peroxide, Betadine® solution and ointment, activated charcoal tablets.

The most important items to include in your canine first aid kit:

Saline

This can be sterile saline purchased from a pharmacy or your veterinarian. This is primarily used for bathing or flushing wounds. It can also be used to flush the eyes. Alternatively saline can be made by dissolving three teaspoons of table salt in a litre of water. This is not as good, since it is not a sterile solution. It is, however acceptable in an emergency situation.

Large Syringe

These should be at least 20ml and do not need to have a needle attached. You should be able to purchase one of these from a pharmacy or your veterinarian. This can be used to draw up the saline and inject it into wounds to flush them out. Saline from a syringe can also be used cautiously to flush the eyes where they have been contaminated with an irritating substance. You can use a syringe to give your dog some water if you feel that they are dehydrated or are not drinking enough. Smaller syringes are also useful for giving liquid medications orally and occasionally rectally.

Non-adherent dressings

Cotton and cloth bandages will adhere to open wounds and make removing the bandages very painful and difficult. Non-adherent dressings can be applied to open wounds to prevent this from happening. A soft dressing is then applied on top of this.

Roll cotton

This is used to bandage wounds and is available in various widths. It holds the non-adherent dressing against the wound and also absorbs secretions such as blood, discharge and bacteria taking them away from the wound. It will also serve to partially immobilise the area and pads the wound, protecting it from further trauma. By spreading the forces out, this layer helps prevent the other layers from digging in too much.

Conforming gauze dressing

This is used above roll cotton dressings to help hold the bandage in place and give some degree of firmness. Conforming gauze can be either rigid or have some degree of elasticity and is available in various widths. I prefer products with some elasticity.

Adhesive bandage

This is used over the gauze bandage to hold the whole dressing in place. Because these types of bandages are very sticky they can be difficult to unravel. This means that they are difficult to apply without inadvertently making them too tight. To avoid this, before you apply such bandages you should unravel them completely and then re-roll them.

Unrolling and re-rolling adhesive bandage.

Tape

There are many different types of tape which you can use to help hold bandages or splints in place. You can also use tape with cotton wool or gauze, with some Betadine® (povidone iodine) ointment to make bandaids. When you use tape you should fold the free end on itself to make a little tab. This will make it far easier to remove. The best type for your kit is probably a clear tape that is not too sticky rather than a very adhesive cloth tape that is harder to remove.

Gauze swabs

These are square pieces of gauze that are available in various sizes. They are useful for wiping and cleaning or to apply pressure to areas of bleeding. You can also fold them up and use these with some tape to create bandaids for your dog.

Thermometer

These can be glass or digital and should only be used rectally. Digital thermometers are much more convenient, quicker and easier to use and read.

KY® or water-based lubricant jelly

This is required to lubricate the tip of the thermometer before use. You can also use sterile KY or other water-based lubricant jelly (from a previously unopened sterile tube) to fill open wounds before applying a dressing. This helps to prevent contamination with hair and dirt.

Tick removers

The two major types are ones with a tweezer type action and one that hooks under the tick. Both work using a twisting action. Either type is acceptable, however, personally I find that the ones that hook under the tick are much easier to use. You can purchase these from your veterinarian or a pet store.

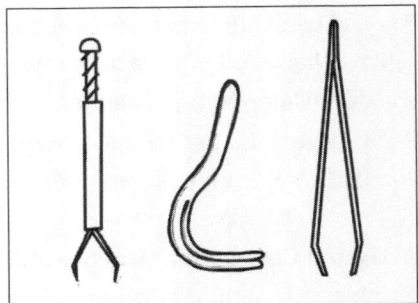

Tick removers and tweezers.

Tweezers or forceps

These can be useful to remove small objects embedded in your dog's skin such as obvious splinters, small pieces of glass, insect stingers and ticks or grass seeds. Anything beyond this really needs to be removed by your veterinarian.

Scissors

These are useful for cutting the bandages and tapes. They should have rounded tips to avoid cutting your dog accidentally.

Gloves

Latex examination gloves are not sterile, however they help to reduce contamination of wounds with the natural bacteria on your hands. They also protect you from coming into contact with blood and other body fluid.

Soda crystals

These are crystals of sodium carbonate. They are useful for inducing vomiting and are very safe. They can be purchased from a pharmacy or a supermarket in the laundry detergent aisle.

Hydrogen peroxide

You can use a three per cent solution to safely induce vomiting. Most preparations available from the supermarket or pharmacy are this concentration. You can dilute more concentrated solutions to three per cent. For example if you have a 10 per cent solution you can use one part of this solution to two parts water to make approximately a three per cent solution.

Activated Charcoal tablets or solution

These can sometimes be useful to bind toxins in the gut that your dog has ingested. You can purchase these from a pharmacy.

Betadine® (povidone iodine 10 per cent) solution or ointment

This is a relatively safe antiseptic that may be helpful, for example when bathing the umbilical cords of newly born pups. Betadine® ointment can also be used on bandaids as an antiseptic. You should not use other antiseptics such as Dettol® as they can be very harmful to dogs' skin. No antiseptic should be left in contact with the skin for prolonged periods.

For more information on your dog's first aid kit contents see: www.firstaidfordogs.com.au

Any medications that your dog has been prescribed for an emergency situation should be included in your kit. Examples of these would include an adrenaline pen if your dog suffers anaphylaxis (a severe life threatening allergic reaction) after bee stings. If your dog is a diabetic it is important to have a source of sugar easily available such as honey or corn syrup. If your dog is being treated for Cushing's disease your veterinarian may have prescribed corticosteroids to be administered in emergencies. Similarly if your dog has Addison's disease you may have instructions to give additional corticosteroids in an emergency.

There is further advice on how to use these items throughout this book.

You will notice that I have not included any pain relief medications in the first aid kit. The majority of pain relief medications used in dogs are either NSAIDs—non-steroidal anti-inflammatory drugs (similar to aspirin) or opiates such as morphine. As is the case with all drugs, NSAIDs not only have beneficial effects but can also have negative side effects including causing stomach ulcers. These negative side effects are accentuated in certain circumstances such as if your dog is dehydrated. Some other medications will interact with NSAIDs and they should not be given concurrently. For these reasons I do not recommend that you keep NSAIDs in your dog's first aid kit. Also NSAIDs specifically designed for use in dogs are much safer and easier to dose accurately than those registered for humans. If your dog has been prescribed an NSAID you may be able to use this in an emergency situation if your veterinarian has given you guidelines to do so.

Although when used properly opiates are relatively safe and effective pain killers, they are rarely prescribed for use at home as they are highly regulated drugs. Consequently they are not available for your dog's first aid kit. Paracetamol is an over-the-counter drug that people often use for pain relief. Dogs are **much** more sensitive to it than people are and require **much** smaller doses. As a result you should not administer paracetamol to your dog unless you are specifically directed to by a veterinarian.

Recognising Serious Emergencies

Owners often find it very hard to know whether their dog is having an emergency. They are consequently faced with the dilemma of whether they should seek veterinary attention or not. You may be left wondering whether the problem can wait until the morning, until Monday or after a public holiday. Dogs are like young children in that they cannot tell us that that they are unwell, instead we have to rely on how they behave to let us know. As a result dogs can be very sick by the time we realise that they have a problem. In addition animals will attempt to hide their illness and pain as a preservation reflex. You know your dog better than anyone else, so in general, if you are worried about your dog it indicates that you should seek veterinary attention. It is far better to see or speak to a veterinarian and have the peace of mind rather than continue to worry and potentially have your dog's condition deteriorate.

It is impossible to say exactly which circumstances are definite emergencies that require immediate attention. This chapter provides a guide to which circumstances are more likely to indicate a serious emergency.

Bleeding

Excessive bleeding, regardless of the cause constitutes an emergency. This may be a result of a traumatic injury and is especially a problem if it is spurting or cannot be stopped by applying direct pressure. Bleeding can also occur in the gut and be present in vomit or stools. Blood may discolour the urine indicating either bleeding or another potentially serious problem. Dogs may cough blood or they may start bleeding from the nose. A problem with blood clotting can cause bleeding in any part of the body.

Trauma

Any severe trauma such as a road traffic accident, dog fight or a large fall warrants veterinary attention even if the dog involved appears normal. This is because some injuries may be internal or hidden by fur. Some injuries will also not become obvious until some time after the trauma. It is especially important to seek immediate veterinary attention if the trauma causes obvious bleeding, severe injuries such as broken bones or exposed internal organs, difficulty breathing, paralysis, pain or altered consciousness.

Difficulty breathing

Difficulty breathing when your animal is resting is always an emergency. There are many causes of difficulty breathing and it is often hard to determine what is causing the problem. Dogs with difficulty breathing can often become very distressed which further contributes to the problem. It is important to keep your dog as calm as possible. Keep them out of the heat and take them to a veterinarian as soon as you can.

Vomiting and diarrhoea

Vomiting and diarrhoea can be emergency situations but they are not always. Dogs have a very strong vomiting reflex and often vomit when there is only a minor upset. These signs are more likely to indicate an emergency if they are severe, progress rapidly or continue for longer than 24-36 hours. Continued vomiting or diarrhoea will eventually lead to dehydration and so will require veterinary intervention. If the vomit or diarrhoea is large in volume or is very frequent, dehydration is more likely to occur. Vomiting is more likely to lead to dehydration if your dog cannot even hold down water. If your dog continues to vomit even after you have taken their food away this is potentially serious.

If your dog becomes depressed and generally sick accompanying vomiting or diarrhoea this indicates that the problem is an emergency. Similarly if your dog also has a fever it indicates a more serious problem. Abdominal pain also indicates that the problem is more likely to be an emergency.

Signs of pain include whimpering or groaning, turning around and looking at their belly, hunching in the hind limbs and arching the lower back or bowing down onto the forelimbs. Your dog may show these signs if you try to touch their belly or pick them up.

If your dog's vomit contains fresh blood or the appearance of coffee grounds, which also indicates gut bleeding, this is also likely to be an emergency situation. Similarly, black or bloody feces also indicates bleeding into the gut and is likely to indicate a serious problem.

If you are concerned that your dog's condition is complicated by any of the conditions described in this section you should take them to a veterinarian. You should also take them to a veterinarian if they are young (less than 1 year) or elderly (older than 8 years) or if they have another medical condition.

Abdominal bloating

Abdominal distension or bloating often indicates a serious problem. This is especially true in large dogs where it may indicate bloat, a build up of gas in the stomach, which can actually twist on itself and become blocked. This is an urgent emergency and can sometimes be fatal, you need to take your dog straight to a veterinary surgery. In other serious conditions the abdomen can become distended with fluid. Where the belly has swollen or become distended rapidly it is most likely an emergency situation and you should take your dog to a veterinarian as soon as possible. There are other non-emergency conditions that can make the belly appear distended such as a slow build up of abdominal fat.

Weakness, collapse and paralysis

There are many causes of weakness and collapse, however whenever this occurs this is likely to indicate a serious problem and so veterinary attention should be sought immediately. These conditions can sometimes be episodic. Even if your dog appears to have recovered completely, please do not discount this. Such episodes really need to be investigated by your veterinarian. Severe depression and unconsciousness are also emergencies.

Similarly there are many causes of paralysis including tick paralysis, snake bites, blood clots, poisonings, tumours and spinal problems like slipped discs, fractures and dislocations. Regardless of the cause, paralysis is always serious and timely treatment is essential. If you suspect a spinal problem you should use a supporting board as described on page 55.

Fits

Like humans, dogs can have fits or convulsions and these can occur for many reasons. They may be as simple as episodes of staring into space or twitching of facial muscles. However, they are often much more dramatic than this and can involve unconsciousness, repeated violent limb movements, frothing at the mouth and are frequently accompanied by urination and defecation. A seizure in itself is of minimal harm as long as it does not go on for longer than 90 seconds. Seizures become very dangerous if they go on much longer than this or if they occur one after the other. In either of these cases veterinary assistance should be sought immediately. Also dogs can harm themselves during a seizure. If your dog has just had its first mild seizure it is important to see a veterinarian as soon as possible to try to find out why it happened. If your dog has already been diagnosed with a seizure disorder then a single short seizure may not be a reason to rush them to a veterinarian.

Poisoning

If you know that your dog has ingested a poisonous substance or potentially had exposure to one this is definitely a reason to seek veterinary assistance. Early intervention can make a huge difference. See Poisonings on page 62 for more information regarding specific poisons. Likewise, if you suspect that your dog has been bitten by a snake or poisonous spider, they should be taken to a see a veterinarian.

Allergic reactions

Acute allergic reactions can produce many symptoms in dogs, including facial swelling. This can become a problem if it starts to compromise breathing and so should be treated promptly. Allergic reactions can also cause intense itchiness. If this is severe dogs can scratch so much that they cause a lot of damage to themselves. If your dog is very itchy and starting to damage themselves you should seek veterinary attention.

Severe reactions can sometimes cause vomiting, diarrhoea and collapse. If you suspect that any of these symptoms are caused by allergic reactions you should take your dog to a veterinarian immediately.

Urinary blockage

Failure to urinate can also indicate a serious problem. This may indicate a blockage to the urethra and is much more likely to occur in male dogs. Your dog may try to urinate without producing anything or only a few drops, perhaps contaminated with blood. They may strain or even cry out when they are trying to urinate. Initially your dog may try to urinate frequently but as they become sicker they may give up trying to urinate all together. Often they will lick their genitals excessively which may make them inflamed. If the urinary blockage continues, toxins cannot be excreted and will start to build up. The bladder can become stretched and damaged or even burst. You should not try to feel for the bladder as it may be very tight and easily burst. If you suspect that your dog has a urinary blockage they should be seen by your veterinarian immediately. If you need to carry your dog, do so by lifting your dog from behind their hind legs rather than under their belly so you do not place extra pressure on the bladder.

Hyperthermia, fever and hypothermia

Many factors can influence your dog's temperature. However, if it is greater than 40°C or less than 37°C, this indicates an emergency situation that requires intervention. See Hyperthermia and Hypothermia page 93 for more information.

Vaginal discharge and uterine infections

Uterine infections can be life threatening. They can occur in older bitches who have not been spayed. They generally become apparent a couple of weeks to a month after a heat cycle. An affected bitch may have a foul smelling bloody or pussy discharge from their vulva. This may be hard to notice as she may lick this off and will generally lick her vulva more. She may have a fever, poor appetite and be more lethargic. She may drink and urinate more and, in some cases, will be lame. This condition is an emergency and she should be seen by a veterinarian immediately.

Eye problems

The eyes are very delicate and precious. Any problem with the eyes is potentially an emergency and time is of the essence. Problems with the eyes can be indicated by a sudden change in their appearance such as swelling, redness, cloudiness, a blue tinge or filling with blood. An eye problem may be painful which is indicated by excessive blinking or holding the eyelids shut. Excessive discharge can also indicate a problem. It is especially important to see a veterinarian if the eye has become painful subsequent to trauma such as a fight with a cat or running into a stick or bush. If a poison has entered your dog's eyes it should be flushed out thoroughly. You should also contact the Poison Information Centre (see page 111) and take your dog to a veterinarian as soon as possible. Timely treatment is vital with eye problems to avoid long term problems like blindness.

Puppies and elderly dogs

Like babies, puppies are much more fragile than mature dogs. Whenever puppies become sick there is always the potential for them to deteriorate very quickly. If your puppy is unwell they should be seen by a veterinarian as soon as possible. Similarly elderly animals (older than eight years) and animals with other medical issues such as diabetes can become very sick very quickly.

Preventing Emergencies

Unfortunately a lot of emergencies will be completely beyond your control and will occur regardless of what you do. However, there are many things that you can do to help prevent emergencies involving your dog. Keeping your dog restricted to your property will help reduce the chance of them being hit by a car, attacked by other dogs or suffering malicious acts by people not as sympathetic to our canine friends. Having your dogs desexed will reduce their tendency to wander and will help reduce aggression towards other dogs. It can also prevent or reduce some medical problems such as uterine infections, breast cancer and some prostate problems. When you are walking your dog on the street you should always keep them on a lead. Many owners do not do this because they believe that their dog is trustworthy and streetwise. However, all dogs are still animals and will behave in unpredictable ways, especially when they are scared or in pain. If frightened even the most sensible dog may run out dangerously onto a road.

Having identification on your dog means that if they do become lost, they are more easily returned to you before they suffer any harm. All dogs should wear a collar with a tag and your contact details. You may also wish to have your veterinarian's contact details on this so they can be taken there if they are sick or injured. Your dog should also be microchipped. This is a legal requirement of owning pet dogs and involves implanting a tiny electronic identification device under the skin, usually around the neck area. Each microchip has a unique number, which is stored with your dog's and your details at several central registers. Veterinarians and pounds can then identify your dog by waving a special microchip reader over your dog. It is vital that you keep these details current to avoid any problems contacting you if your dog is found. You should contact your local council to check or change these details.

Feeding

Other than your dog's general preventative medicine regime, including regular vaccination, heartworm prevention and intestinal worm and flea control: the major influence that you have over their health is the way that you feed them. There is great controversy concerning the ideal diet for dogs. It is not the purpose of this book to suggest whether one diet is better than another one. Instead I will give some general advice on feeding practices that can help prevent emergencies.

Pancreatitis

Pancreatitis is inflammation of the pancreas, a small spongy organ that sits next to the stomach and small intestine. The pancreas has a very important role in secreting enzymes to help digestion as well as secreting hormones such as insulin. Pancreatitis causes nausea, vomiting, abdominal pain and lethargy. The severity of pancreatitis ranges from a relatively mild condition to a devastating, life threatening condition. The exact cause of pancreatitis in dogs is unknown. There is, however, a strong association with large amounts of fat in the diet, especially in one large fatty meal. Because of this, it is important to avoid your dog having access to fatty foods such as fatty bones, meat trimmings or barbecues. This disease tends to occur more often around festive periods and public holidays when people are having parties and their dogs have access to such foods. This can be a recurrent problem. If your dog has previously had pancreatitis it is especially important that you avoid excessive fat in their diet on a long term basis. Obesity is also thought to be a risk factor.

Eating bones

Many owners like to include bones in their dog's diet. Most dogs love bones and they have obvious benefits for their teeth. Unfortunately bones can have devastating consequences if they become stuck in the food pipe. Types of bones most likely to become stuck are those that are small enough to be swallowed whole. The exact type of bone that would potentially be a problem varies with your dog's size but bones which are commonly a problem are brisket bones and neck bones. As a general rule, bones that can fit whole in your dog's mouth are more likely to be a problem. Bones are more likely to become stuck if your dog is a greedy eater and certainly this a common trait of some breeds such as Labrador Retrievers, Beagles and Corgies. I have seen dogs that have eaten what I would consider to be risky bones all of their lives with no problems, then have a bone become stuck as an older dog, sometimes with tragic consequences. Just because your dog has not had a problem in the past does not mean that they will never do so. It just means they have been lucky.

If your dog does have a bone stuck, they will have difficulty swallowing it and may seem distressed at the time. They may or may not stop eating. If they continue to eat they will probably regurgitate soon afterwards. Regurgitation involves bringing up undigested food and secretions seemingly effortlessly with minimal or no abdominal contractions. If your dog has a bone stuck in their food pipe they may also gag, retch and swallow excessively. They may drool and have very bad breath. Either as soon as the bone is swallowed or after the bone has been lodged there for several days, it may cause difficulty breathing. This is a very serious complication and requires immediate veterinary attention. If you suspect that your dog has a bone or other object stuck in their food pipe, you should take your dog to a veterinarian as soon as possible as this can quickly become a life threatening problem.

I recommend feeding very large, uncut, raw bones. For a large dog bones such as a beef thigh bones are suitable. Smaller dogs may be able to have a beef or lamb shank. Dogs that can aggressively break off large pieces of bone may not be able to have bones at all since they risk one of these pieces becoming stuck. Cooked bones are brittle and sharp pieces break off easily so these should not be fed. Excessive consumption of bones can also lead to constipation or even an obstructed bowel. The marrow is very fatty and can cause weight gain or even pancreatitis if eaten. The point of feeding bones is so that they can chew on them rather than ingest large amounts of them.

Bloat

Another life threatening condition related to feeding is bloat. Here the dog's stomach becomes distended with food and gas and can actually twist on itself. The exact reason why this occurs is still not known and there are numerous factors involved. It is much more likely to occur in middle aged to older, large breed, deep-chested dogs such as Great Danes and German Shepherds. Signs of bloat include rapid distension of the abdomen, especially on the left hand side, non productive retching, drooling, progressive weakness and eventually collapse. This condition is an emergency and if you suspect this you should take your dog to a veterinarian immediately. Ways that you can reduce the chance of this occurring include:

- feeding several smaller meals rather than one large meal each day
- not allowing access to large amounts of stored food.
- reducing stress during feeding - in multiple dog households you may need to separate dogs during feeding.
- avoid exercising your dog within an hour before or two hours after feeding.
- not allowing your dog to drink large volumes of water at one time, especially after exercising. Instead you should give them small amounts frequently.
- not feeding your dog from an elevated feeding bowl as this may promote the ingestion of air.

There is a hereditary component to bloat. You should ask whether any of the close relatives have had this condition before buying a pup. You should not breed from affected animals.

Swallowed objects

Dogs are inquisitive and tend to chew on various objects and   sometimes swallow them. Some of these will not cause a problem and will eventually be passed. Others have the potential to cause a gastrointestinal obstruction and are very dangerous. Vomiting is the most common signs of an obstruction. Whether a particular object will pass or not varies between dogs. However some are less likely to be passed than others. Some objects that are less likely to be passed include corn cobs, mango or avocado seeds, some toys, balls, rocks and some bones. Long objects such as pantyhose, ribbon or string are very likely to cause an obstruction as they can cause the intestines to become bunched up on themselves. It is very important to keep such objects out of your dog's reach. This is especially important if your dog has a tendency to pick up and chew or swallow such objects. If you suspect that your dog has ingested a foreign object you should take them to your veterinarian straight away. If they have a string or ribbon protruding from their mouth or anus you should not pull on this. To do so may cause internal injury.

Other objects that dogs will chew and swallow, which can potentially cause a problem are sharp objects such as fish hooks and meat skewers, both wooden and metal. These objects are often particularly appealing to dogs when they are covered with bait or meat so special care to keep them away from dogs is warranted. Particularly curious dogs will also ingest sewing needles and pins. If you suspect that your dog has ingested a sharp object you should take them to your veterinarian as soon as possible. If your dog ingests a sharp object with a string attached, such as a fishing hook or a sewing needle, it is always tempting to pull on the string if it is protruding from their mouth or anus. This is not a good idea. Pulling on such a string has the potential to cause internal injury and make the object far harder for a veterinarian to remove. Instead, you should take your dog directly to your veterinarian.

It is also very important to keep poisons, including prescription and over-the-counter preparations, out of your dog's reach. Poisons such as snail and slug bait, rat and mouse bait and cockroach bait are sometimes advertised as 'pet friendly' or 'pet safe'. In my experience these are sometimes still potentially harmful to dogs. You should store them away from dogs and seriously consider whether the risk is worth using them at all. This will be discussed further in Poisonings on page 62.

Sticks

Many dogs love chasing and fetching sticks. Unfortunately throwing sticks for your dog can sometimes be very dangerous. Occasionally sticks will land digging into the ground pointing towards your fast oncoming dog. If your dog is particularly unlucky they can impale themselves on the stick. Chewing on sticks can also be harmful because splinters may become embedded in your dog's mouth or throat.

You should not throw sticks for your dog and you should discourage them from chewing on them.

Heatstroke and hypothermia

heatstroke is caused by an elevated body temperature and is a very serious condition with potentially devastating consequences. It is usually caused by hot days combined with vigorous activity. Some dogs of athletic or working breeds, such as Kelpies or Border Collies, may cope very well with these conditions and not have a problem. Conversely dogs of less athletic breeds, especially those with short noses, such as Bulldogs are much more likely to overheat. I do not recommend excessive exercise on hot days for any dog but this is especially important for less athletic dogs. Dogs left in cars on hot days are at serious risk of suffering heatstroke, even with a window open.

Very small dogs and puppies are at risk of becoming cold when they are outside in cold weather. Older dogs (more than 8 years old) may also be at risk. You should consider giving them a warm coat to wear.

Noise phobia

Some dogs become very distressed by loud noises like thunder or fireworks. If they become very upset, some dogs will run away and risk being hit by motor vehicles, running through glass windows, falling off a cliff or coming to some other harm. I have also seen one dog that became so distressed by a thunder storm that she ran around madly until she collapsed with severe heatstroke. If your dog suffers from noise phobia it is important to try to minimise the impact of the problem. You can do this by discussing behaviour modification techniques with your veterinarian. At least in the initial stages of the problem it may be important to use sedatives in anticipation of a noisy event or during an episode to help prevent your dog hurting themselves. You can discuss the use of appropriate sedatives with your veterinarian.

Tick paralysis

Paralysis ticks are common on the east coast of Australia and can attach to dogs. As their name suggests they can cause life threatening paralysis. When ticks attach they can be very small (less than 1mm) so they can be hard to detect. Dogs have coats which can make ticks very difficult to find. There are several products on the market that help prevent tick attachment. None, however, completely guarantees against this or against paralysis. The best defence against tick paralysis in your dog is to perform regular manual searches of their skin. Although tick paralysis can occur at any time of the year it is most important to perform regular searches at the height of the season, from Spring to Autumn. You can make finding ticks much easier by having long-haired breeds clipped short.

Electrocution

Electrocution is a serious condition that can sometimes occur when dogs chew on electrical cords. Puppies are much more likely to do this than adult dogs. Electrical safety switches can be very beneficial. You can try to prevent electrocution by keeping electrical cords out of your dog's reach. You can also unplug electrical cords when they are not in use. Covering the cords with protective sleeves, which you can purchase from electrical stores can also be helpful. Giving your dogs plenty of toys to chew on is a good way to distract them from chewing electrical cords.

Medication

It is not uncommon for owners of dogs receiving regular medication to run out of medication over a weekend or holiday period. Not giving certain medications, such as those to control heart disease or epilepsy, can have devastating consequences. It is very important that you always have a good supply of your dog's regular medication, especially before a period when your veterinary clinic is closed.

Assessing the Canine Emergency Patient

When a person is an emergency patient, the most common course of action is for bystanders to administer first aid while they wait for an ambulance service to arrive. One reason for this is to leave moving the person to the professionals and so avoid causing further injury. This also means that professional care is available on the way to a hospital. Unfortunately there is no organised animal ambulance service. This means that in most cases dog owners or bystanders have to provide both first aid and transport for the patient. As a result the emphasis should then be on transporting the dog, as quickly and carefully as possible, to a veterinary hospital where proper facilities are available to treat them effectively. Occasionally a veterinarian may be able to attend the scene or provide transport.

Safety

When dealing with a canine emergency your first priority should be to identify danger to yourself, other people, and then the injured dog. You can potentially become seriously injured trying to assist a dog. If this happens it adds another complication to the situation and does not help the victim at all. Often the source of the dog's injury remains a danger to it and others. Examples of dangers include traffic if the dog is on a road, the other dogs if the dog has been a victim of a dog fight, live wires may still pose a risk if the dog has been electrocuted or a fire may threaten the safety of the scene. The victim themselves can also be a danger to you or other people on the scene.

Hit by a car

A dog that has been hit by a car in the middle of a busy road is at risk of being hit again and so are the people trying to help it. This is especially dangerous at night or in bad weather when vision is impaired. Don't approach the dog until there is a break in traffic. If you can, send someone up the street to try to stop oncoming traffic. The priority must be to move the dog off the road as carefully as possible to remove yourself and the dog from further danger.

Dog fights

A dog or dogs that are attacking another dog represent a serious danger to those trying to separate them as well as any bystanders. Any attempt to separate them can be very dangerous and you do so at your own risk. You should avoid placing any of your body parts between two fighting dogs as you may be bitten. There are some techniques that may help separate a dog that is firmly biting down on its victim. Probably the safest method is to distract the dogs. This can be done using your voice or by wetting them with a hose or bucket of water. If they are wearing a lead you can pull on this. Pulling on a collar is probably too dangerous as it puts your hands near their mouth. Another tactic is to attack the dog that you perceive to be the primary aggressor. This is probably the most dangerous course of action as it is the most likely to cause the attacker to turn on you. If you do chose this method using makeshift weapons or kicking with an outstretched leg is probably the least dangerous option (remember not to be too brutal even if they do have your beloved pooch in their grasp). If the primary offender is not castrated, grabbing and pulling on their scrotum may cause them to let go. One other less

If you do not feel safe or confident separating fighting dogs, DO NOT attempt to. Call your local council ranger or the police. See page 111 for Emergency contacts.

savoury technique is to insert one of your fingers into the primary attacker's anus in an attempt to make them release their grip. Unless they are properly restrained the attacking dog (or dogs) remains a threat to the victim and any assistants even after the dogs are separated.

Electrocution and fires

If the dog you are trying to help has been electrocuted it is vital that you are not also electrocuted. There may still be live wires around, perhaps that the victim has chewed through. Before approaching the animal you should turn off the power and unplug any possibly live cables. If this is not possible you should use a long wooden pole, such as a broom stick, to move any live wires away from the victim before approaching them. Similarly, you should not risk becoming trapped in a fire while trying to help a canine emergency victim. You should move yourself and the victim well away from any fire and out of danger before administering first aid.

Approaching sick or injured dogs—even if not your own

Sick or injured dogs are often very scared and in pain. This can make even the most friendly and trusted pet aggressive and a danger to the person attending to them. It is very important to avoid being bitten when you are trying to help them. Approach the dog very slowly and avoid any sudden movements. Watch their body language and look for warning signs including:

- growling
- snarling the upper lip
- raised hackles

Take notice of these warnings and stop approaching a dog that is potentially aggressive. Note that some dogs showing signs of aggression may continue to wag their tail before they become aggressive. Very submissive dogs that are rolling on their back may be very scared and bite suddenly out of fear.

If the dog is relatively receptive, calmly introduce yourself by offering the back of your hand under their chin for them to smell. Do not approach them from above or behind them as they may be threatened by this. Similarly avoid direct eye contact as some dogs may find this threatening. Always make sure that the dog can see you before you touch them, so that they are not taken by surprise. Talk to them quietly and calmly, ideally using their name. If you do not know the dog you may be able to find their name on their collar tag. Squatting next to them can make you seem less threatening than if you are standing over them. However you should not sit down next to them as you may not be able to move away quickly enough if they do become aggressive.

Muzzles

You can try to use a muzzle before you attempt to examine or treat a dog that is in pain and may potentially bite. This actually often makes the animal calmer and I think feel more secure. However, some dogs will become aggressive while you are trying to apply a muzzle and in this case you should leave the examination to a veterinarian. Muzzles can be made of leather, nylon or be plastic or metal cage type muzzles. Alternatively you can fashion a home made cloth muzzle as shown below. If your dog has a short nose

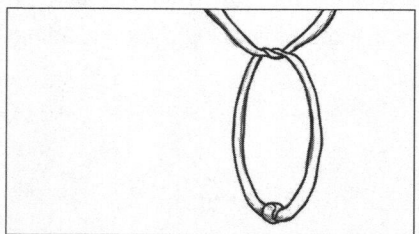 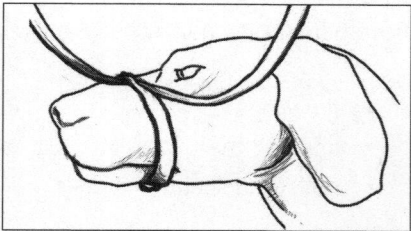

you will need to purchase a special type of muzzle. It is important that the muzzle fits well. You should never fully rely on any muzzle however, as there is always the chance that a dog will escape. It can be dangerous to the dog to use a muzzle if the dog is vomiting or having trouble breathing. You will have to consider your safety as well as the risks to the dog when deciding whether or not to use a muzzle. Cage type muzzles are less dangerous as they interfere less with breathing and if the dog does vomit it can drain.

Making and fitting a home made cloth muzzle

1. Take a long piece of cloth such as gauze, a necktie or pantyhose and tie a large knot in the middle of it.
2. Make a loop in the cloth, this should be large enough to fit over your dog's nose.
3. Coming from above and behind your dog's head, slip the loop over your dog's nose and tighten it. This should be firm but not so tight that it disrupts blood supply or breathing. The large knot in the cloth should sit between the bones of the dog's lower jaw to help anchor it.
4. Bring the loose ends under the jaw and cross them. Now take them behind the dog's head, being careful not to include the ears.
5. Tie the loose ends firmly behind the head.

Often dogs are in too much pain for you to do anything to help them or even appreciate the extent of their injuries. Instead you should pick them up carefully, to avoid hurting them or being bitten yourself, and transport

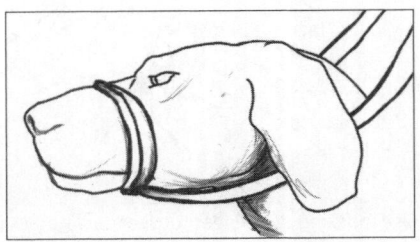
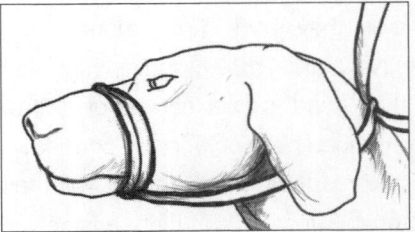

them to a veterinarian. If you suspect hind limb injury you should hold them around their belly rather than their hind limbs. If you suspect a back injury you should transport them on a spinal supporting board, as described on page 55. Sometimes throwing a sheet, blanket or towel over a dog that is being aggressive due to pain can help you pick them up more safely. You can also wrap them in this to help reduce contamination of their wounds and protect your car and clothes from blood.

Assessing the canine patient's responsiveness

Once you have ensured that there is no further danger to yourself, other people or the victim you should assess the collapsed dog's level of consciousness. Try to rouse the dog to see if they are at all responsive, use their name if you know it. If they do respond to you they probably do not require resuscitation at that point and you should assess them for shock, breathing difficulty or injuries. These dogs may be in a very fragile condition and could deteriorate and stop breathing or their heart could stop. You should continue to monitor their condition closely and take them to a veterinary clinic as soon as possible.

If they are not responsive, assess the patient using the acronym **ABC: Airway, Breathing and Circulation.** This helps you remember the most important things to check and what to do for a collapsed patient. Once you have addressed these things you can worry about the animal's other injuries.

Airway

If a collapsed dog is non-responsive, the first thing you should check is that they have and unobstructed airway. You should make sure that their head is in a natural or slightly extended position and not bent down towards their chest. Gently pull their tongue forward to help ensure an

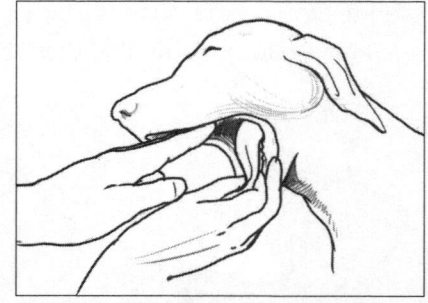

Use index and forefinger to clear airways.

open airway. You should then check their mouth for foreign objects or fluids such as saliva, vomit or blood that may be causing an obstruction. You can use your index and middle fingers in a sweeping action at the back of their mouth to clear this. Do not put your hands in a conscious or fitting dog's mouth as you may be bitten. If there is a large amount of fluid in the mouth you can elevate the hind quarters so that it drains out. This is also useful if the patient has suffered near-drowning and has water in their lungs. A cloth may also be useful to mop up any fluid.

Breathing

Once you have cleared the airway, the next step is to check if the dog is breathing. The best was to do this is put your head next to theirs and look at their chest to see if it is rising and falling. This should only take a second or two. If there is no chest movement or if there are only very, very small movements you will need to breathe for the dog. This is best done by mouth-to-nose breathing. You should close the dog's mouth with one hand and cover the dog's nose with your mouth. Then give two long gentle breaths (1–2 seconds each). Between each breath you should watch the chest fall as the air is exhaled. Dogs are usually much smaller than us and have much smaller lungs. You should only continue the breath until you can start to see their chest expand. Giving breaths that are too large can damage their delicate lungs.

You should then watch the chest again to see if the dog has started breathing for itself. If the dog is still not breathing then you should then start giving breaths at a rate of around 30 breaths per minute or one breath every two seconds. Do not attempt mouth-to-nose breathing on a conscious dog or one that is breathing for itself.

Circulation

The next step is to check the dog's circulation. This means checking if the dog has a heartbeat or a pulse. These can be checked by feeling the heartbeat on the chest wall or feeling for a femoral pulse. You should also check their gum colour, see pages 11–13. This information can give you some idea of whether the animal is suffering shock. In the early stages of shock patients will have an elevated heart and pulse rates (greater than 120 beats per minute). The pulses may feel normal or bounding. The gums will remain a normal pink colour. As shock progresses the pulses will become weaker and the gums may become pale. The dog's temperature may also be reduced and their limbs and ears may feel cool. When shock becomes very advanced, the pulses will be weak, the gums will be pale, the body temperature will be reduced but the heart and pulse rates will be reduced (less than 80 beats per minute). Once shock is this advanced it is very serious and the dog's heart may stop at any time. You should be prepared to start cardiopulmonary resuscitation or CPR as described in the next chapter. Note that pain may resemble early shock. Also shock due to infection may cause elevated heart and pulse rates with brick red gums and an elevated body temperature.

If the dog you are assessing has a heartbeat you should continue to breathe for the dog until they start to breathe on their own again. Continue to monitor their heartbeat or pulses during mouth-to-nose breathing. If there is no pulse or heartbeat, or it stops while you are performing mouth-to-nose breathing you will need to start CPR as described in the next chapter.

Once you have assessed the patient you should assess the scene itself. There may be evidence of a poison that the dog has eaten. See the Poisonings section on page 62 for more details. If a snake bite was the cause there may be a dead snake in the area. See Snake Bites on page 86 for more information on snake bites. There may also be vomit or diarrhoea at the scene.

Cardiopulmonary Resuscitation (CPR)

The major difference between CPR in humans and dogs is that the purpose of CPR in humans is to try to keep the patient alive until ambulance staff can attend. They then continue resuscitation and transport the person to a hospital. As there is no specialised ambulance service for dogs, your major aim is to transport your dog to a veterinary hospital as soon as possible while using CPR to keep them alive in the meantime. A veterinary hospital can provide much more assistance than you can give in the first aid situation. Also, dogs that require CPR often do so repeatedly so there is no point spending valuable time trying to fully resuscitate them at the scene to have them stop breathing or have their heart stop beating again no closer to a veterinary clinic and specialised care. Limited resuscitation can continue in the car on the way to the veterinary clinic. However, as your safety is always foremost, you should always drive carefully and everyone should wear seat belts.

A dog can stop breathing and their heart can stop beating for numerous reasons. It can occur suddenly, for example after they have suffered serious trauma or electrocution. It can also occur as a result of the gradual deterioration of a dog's condition due to another disease. Once you have assessed a collapsed patient and determined that they are non-responsive, are not breathing for themselves and do not have a heartbeat or pulse as described in the previous chapter, you should start Cardiopulmonary Resuscitation (CPR).

If the patient is not breathing on their own you should be giving them mouth-to-nose breathing at approximately 30 breaths per minute as described in the section on Breathing on page 41. Once you have checked the circulation, if there is no heartbeat or pulse you need to start to chest compressions.

There are many different techniques for performing chest compressions. This is largely due to the wide range in size of different dogs as well as controversy regarding which technique is best. You will have to adjust the technique you use based partly on the dogs size and also what you are comfortable with. Dogs less that 7kg can be resuscitated on their sides with you kneeling facing their chest. You should apply firm compressions directly over the heart which is located roughly behind the elbow. You should do this at a rate of around 120 compressions every minute or two compressions every second. The force required for this will vary widely for different dogs. Dogs larger than 7kg should ideally be resuscitated on their back. You should apply firm compressions to the breast bone at a rate of 80–100 compressions every minute. It can be difficult to balance dogs on their back so if you are having difficulty with this you can perform the compressions with them on their side as described for small dogs. To apply the chest compressions your arms should be held out straight with your elbows locked. You should use the palm of one hand to contact the chest and the other should be placed on top of it. You should pivot from your hips to use your body to create the compressions rather than bending your arms. When you perform chest compressions with either technique it is possible to break ribs, this is not the end of the world if it happens, but is preferably avoided. There is a fine balance between being effective and doing damage.

If you are performing the CPR with two people, you should aim to give one breath every 3–5 chest compressions. This breath should be given between compressions and you should ideally do this without a pause in the compressions. The second operator can check how effective you are being by feeling for a femoral pulse. If there is no pulse you can change your technique slightly. You can increase or decrease the compression rate or you could increase or decrease the compression force. You can also look to see if the gum colour

Never perform chest compressions on dogs with a heartbeat or pulse.

is improving. If you have a third person helping they can apply continuous firm pressure to the belly with their hands as this can also increase effectiveness.

If you are performing the CPR alone, you should give two breaths every 15 compressions. You will obviously have to have a pause in the compressions to do this. You should check to see if the dog's heart has started beating on its own by briefly stopping the chest compressions and feeling for a heartbeat or pulse once every minute. If there is no heartbeat or pulse you will have to keep going. If there is a heartbeat or the pulse has returned, continue to monitor this while giving mouth-to-nose breathing at 30 breaths per minute until the dog starts breathing for itself again.

Some people believe that chest compressions alone help move enough air in and out of the lungs. This means that, if the heart has stopped beating, your priority during CPR should be chest compressions rather than breathing. If you are having trouble coordinating them both, the mouth-to-nose breathing should definitely be discontinued first. This is especially true during the first five minutes of CPR after which time breathing also becomes important.

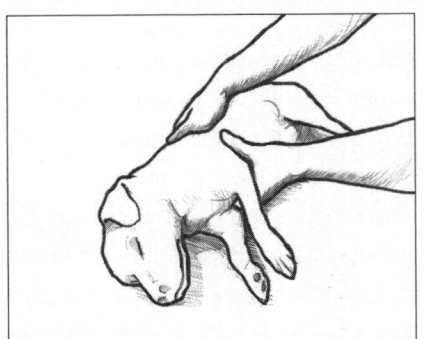

Performing CPR on small dog.

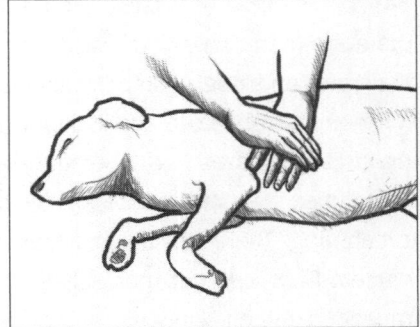

Performing CPR on large dog.

During CPR large amounts of air may build up in the stomach causing it to become very swollen. If this is occurring you can take a few seconds to push on the stomach to try to relieve this.

A dog can stop breathing and its heart stop beating for many reasons. The actual cause to some degree determines the chance of resuscitation efforts being successful. Unfortunately once a dog has stopped breathing, especially if their heart has stopped there is only a small chance that they will ultimately survive. As stated above, this chance is increased by taking them to a veterinary hospital as soon as possible. There is also the chance that if they do recover they will have temporary or permanent neurological problems. However, a small chance makes it very worthwhile trying for those dogs who do survive. If a heartbeat has not been restored after 20 minutes of resuscitation, there is very little chance that the dog will survive the ordeal. If they do survive they are very likely to have severe neurological problems so you should consider discontinuing all efforts after this period.

Trauma

There are many ways your dog can be hurt. Common causes are road traffic accidents and dog fights. Occasionally dogs will fall from great heights or suffer animal abuse. These incidents can cause both external injuries including bruising, grazes and lacerations and internal injuries of varying severity. Sometimes they can cause significant bleeding, which in itself can be life threatening. There can also be bone fractures, dislocations and even spinal injuries. Dogs can cut themselves on sharp objects or have foreign objects imbedded in their skin. They also suffer burns just as we do. Sometimes itchy dogs will damage themselves when they scratch excessively.

Often dogs who have suffered major trauma such as being hit by a car will try to run away. This does not mean that they are not hurt and you should not discount their injuries. They are very scared and confused and are instinctively trying to move away from danger. They may still have life threatening injuries. Any dog that has suffered major trauma should be seen by your veterinarian as soon as possible.

When you are assessing a victim of major trauma it is important to note any difficulty breathing as this may indicate a serious chest injury. Such injuries have the potential to become worse very quickly so you should take your dog to your veterinarian immediately.

Major trauma has the potential to damage the urinary bladder or other parts of the urinary system. It is important to note if your animal has urinated after a traumatic injury. You should also note if the urine is bloody. This is very important information to provide to your veterinarian. The presence of blood in the feces is also potentially significant. Other internal organs can easily be damaged in major trauma. Often these injuries are not apparent for 36–72 hours after the initial injury.

Bleeding

Many different types of injuries can cause bleeding. A graze will often cause a small amount of oozing blood due to capillary damage. Damage to veins will usually cause blood to trickle out. The most serious type of bleeding is from arteries. This causes the most rapid loss of blood and is the hardest to stop. Arterial injury will cause blood to spurt out in pulses. Bleeding that occurs on the outside of the dog's body is usually quite easy to detect. If you detect large amounts of bleeding, the best way to slow or stop this is to apply pressure. You can use gauze swabs from your canine fist aid kit or another piece of cloth, such as clothing or a towel, to apply firm pressure to the source of bleeding. If the gauze cloth becomes soaked in blood do not remove it as this may disturb any blood clots, instead use more gauze or cloth on top of this. Hold this pressure until you can hand your dog into your veterinarian's care or the bleeding stops.

If direct pressure does not control the bleeding, and it continues to spurt from an arterial source, try holding above the wound firmly to block off the supplying artery. If it is continuing to ooze or trickle out, you can try holding just below the wound firmly to try to stop venous blood flow to the wound. These techniques are useful if the bleeding is coming from a limb or the tail. Continue to apply direct pressure to the bleeding wound while doing this.

If this is still not controlling the bleeding from a limb or the tail, you can also try elevating the source of the bleeding above the level of the heart. This works best in large dogs because you can often move the source of the bleeding much higher above the heart than you can with small dogs.

Bleeding can also be internal. It can occur into the chest or into the abdomen and can be very difficult to detect and sometimes is very slow. Bleeding into the chest may cause difficulty breathing. This may or may not be evident initially, sometimes manifesting instead over the 24–36 hours following trauma. Dogs that have bled into their chest may cough up blood. Bleeding into the abdomen may cause some abdominal distention but only if it is severe. It will also cause abdominal pain. Dogs that are bleeding may be in shock, see page 42. There is nothing that you can do about internal bleeding. If you suspect there may be internal bleeding you should rush your dog to your veterinarian immediately.

If your dog is having ANY difficulty breathing they should be taken to a veterinarian immediately.

Skin tears and lacerations

The most common injury received from trauma is damage to the skin and underlying tissue. There may be large tears due to bite wounds or where contact with a car or the ground has torn it off. Road traffic accidents may also cause severe grazes where the skin has come into contact with the road. Sharp edges of fractured bones may cause wounds where they penetrate the skin. Sharp objects can also cut the skin, especially in the pads. Sometimes wounds are much more extensive than they appear externally. With all wounds it is important to minimise further contamination before then dog can be seen by a veterinarian. You should try to stop your dog from licking the wounds. If you have been given an Elizabethan collar (also known as a bucket collar) by your veterinarian for a previous problem you can put this on your dog. These are large plastic collars that project over your dog's head to help prevent them from chewing and licking. Alternatively simply discouraging them from licking should suffice until you can take them to a veterinarian. Wearing latex examination gloves when handling the wound will also help minimise contamination as well as protect you from contact with the dog's blood.

Any wound can become infected so, if there is a delay in seeking veterinary attention, you should flush the wound out using saline (preferably sterile) from a syringe. Do not try to flush or clean a wound that is bleeding profusely as this may encourage further bleeding. Attempt to stop the bleeding instead, as described on page 47. To flush skin wounds, simply fill the syringe with saline and squirt it under reasonable pressure into the wound. You can also gently introduce the tip of a sterile syringe under flaps of skin and squirt saline under these areas.
If there are large amounts of contamination to a wound with hair, dirt, grass or bitumen it may be more useful to pour large volumes of saline onto the wound to wash this off before trying to flush the wound out. Once a wound has been cleaned and flushed, you can then fill the wound with sterile K-Y Jelly® or water-based lubricant to help prevent further contamination.

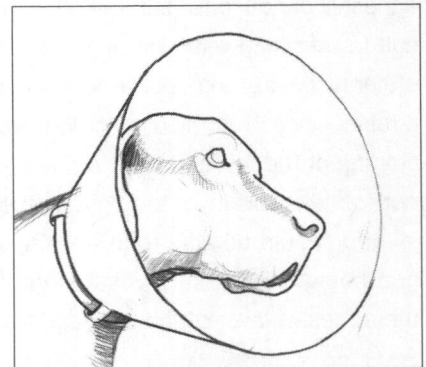

Dog wearing an Elizabethan collar.

The wound can further be protected by applying a light dressing before you see your veterinarian as described on page 50. This can be difficult especially if your dog is in great pain. Only do it if you feel confident and if your dog is not resisting too much. Certain areas on the dog's body can be very difficult to bandage, such as the shoulder, hips and thigh. Consequently, it is often much better to leave the wound management to your veterinarian.

Bandaging wounds

You can bandage wounds on the limbs, including pad injuries or on the body, by firstly gently placing any flaps of skin back down where they normally sit. Dry the area before bandaging the wound. You should then apply a non-adherent dressing over the wound itself. Then apply a layer of roll cotton dressing over this. Each turn of the roll cotton should overlap the previous one by approximately half the width of the bandage. If you are bandaging a limb you should start at the toes and work up. Then apply a layer of conforming gauze over this, again starting at the toes if you are bandaging a limb. This should be firm but not too tight as this can reduce blood supply to the area or interfere with breathing if it is on the body. Again each turn should overlap the previous one by about half the width of the dressing. Finally you can apply the adhesive bandage to help hold this in place. This can be very sticky and difficult to unravel. Before placing the bandage you should unravel it completely, either by having someone else hold onto one end or by sticking the end onto a table. Once unravelled carefully re-roll it. This is applied over the other layers starting at the toe end once more and overlapping each turn. Be very careful not to make this layer too tight as there is generally a tendency to do so.

You should be able to fit two fingers between the bandage and the body part being bandaged. If you cannot it is too tight. You should also continue the adhesive layer of the bandage for about 3–4 cm beyond the other layers

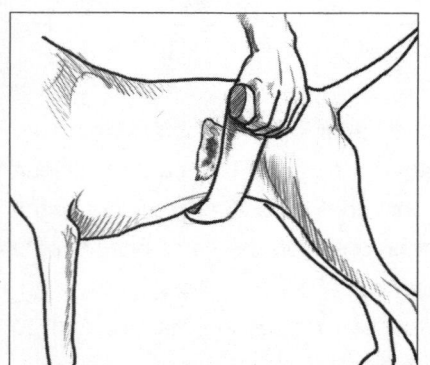 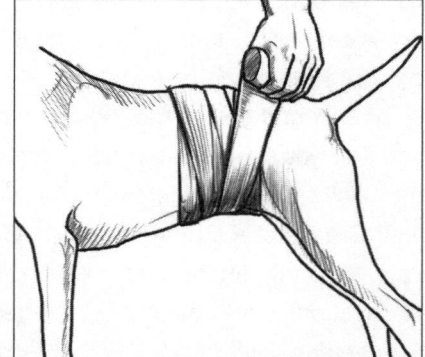

Apply bandage over non-adherent dressing—first cotton roll, then conforming gauze and finally adhesive bandage. Overlap the bandage on each turn by about half its width.

so that it sticks directly to the skin or fur to help hold the bandage on. If you are bandaging the body, sometimes the bandage tends to slip down towards the tail. To try to stop this you should extend the adhesive bandage 3–4cm towards the head beyond the other non-adhesive layers of the bandage.

Ideally any bandage that you have placed should not stay on more than six hours before the animal is checked by a veterinarian. If it does stay on longer than two hours you should check their toes every hour to make sure that they have not become swollen and are still warm. If they are swollen or cold the bandage is cutting off their blood supply and it needs to be removed.

Puncture wounds and embedded foreign objects

Puncture wounds can occur due to injures such as animal bites or a sharp object such as a splinter puncturing the skin. Sometimes the offending object remains embedded in the skin. Puncture wounds, particularly those caused by animal bites, are especially at risk of becoming infected. Animal bites can also cause much more extensive injury than is apparent superficially. Sometimes large amounts of the tissue deep beneath the skin are damaged and the skin may have become detached over a large area although only small puncture wounds may be seen externally. This is often true when a dog picks up and shakes its victim. All puncture wounds should be examined by your veterinarian.

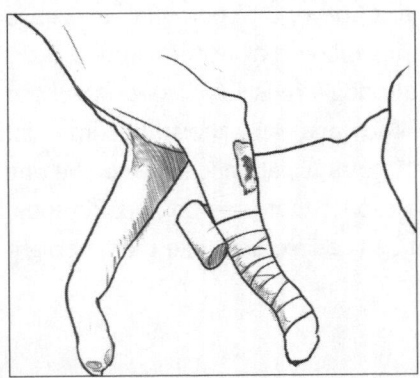

On a limb start at the toes and work up.

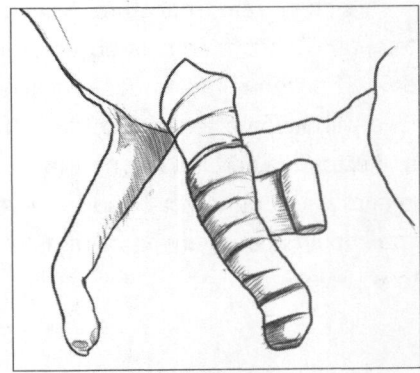

Be careful not to apply the any layer too tightly, especially the adhesive bandage.

If there is any foreign material embedded in the skin, such as a piece of glass or a splinter, try to gently remove this with some tweezers. If it breaks off in the skin leave this for your veterinarian to remove. If the object is a fish hook you should take your dog to a veterinarian immediately. If there is going to be a delay, do not try to pull it out as the barb will prevent this. Instead, if the hook is only shallow you can try to push the hook in further so that the barb exits the skin. You can then carefully cut the exposed barb off using pliers and gently pull the hook out the way it went in. If the hook is embedded deeply into the skin you should leave removing it to your veterinarian.

Any puncture wound should then be flushed out using large amounts of saline (preferably sterile) from a syringe. If the wound is on the pad it may be easier to soak the wound in saline by submersing the whole foot.

Sometimes, if a puncture wound is missed or even if once was treated appropriately, there is the potential for it to become infected and for an abscess to form. Abscesses are collections of puss that appear as soft swellings around the wound site. They can make your dog quite sick, causing a fever, reduced appetite, pain and lethargy. If the abscess ruptures, foul smelling puss, often tinged with blood will ooze out. You can use sterile saline to further flush this out. All abscesses should be checked by your veterinarian.

Although rare, puncture wounds also have the potential to cause tetanus. This is a serious but treatable condition that occurs around 5-10 days after the injury. In this condition the dog's muscles, especially of the face will become tense and hard. The limbs and tail will also become stiff and extended and the dog may fall over. This especially occurs when the dog is stimulated by touch or noise. If you suspect that your dog has tetanus, you should keep them as calm as quiet as possible and take them straight to your veterinarian.

Broken bones

Dogs that are victims of traumatic incidents may also suffer broken bones (or fractures) and dislocations. These can be contained within the body or the fractured ends of the bone can be become externalised through the skin. This makes external fractures relatively easy to identify. Internal fractures may be suspected if there is acute, non-weight bearing lameness in the affected limb after trauma. The limb may be held in an abnormal position. There may be obvious instability of the limb at the site of the fracture where it swings unnaturally. Ultimately an X-ray is needed to identify a fracture. Bone injuries are very painful so you should not try to replace externalised fracture ends, realign the limb or manipulate the area in any way. Doing so has the potential to do further damage.

Bone fractures are very serious and you should take your animal to a veterinarian as soon as possible. You should minimise contamination of any externalised fractures as bone infections can be very serious. When handling an external fracture you should wear examination gloves. If there is going to be a delay in seeing a veterinarian, the wound can be flushed with saline (ideally sterile) from a syringe to help remove any hair or dirt. You can then fill the wound with sterile, water-based, lubricant jelly (ideally from a previously unopened packet) to help prevent further contamination. Over this you can then apply a sterile, non-adherent dressing to the wound.

The next priority is to help immobilise the limb in an attempt to avoid further damage. You can do this by applying an immobilising bandage to the affected limb in the position that you find it. To be effective, your bandage should prevent movement in the joint above and below the fracture. If you do not immobilise both joints the movement in those joints will mean that the bandage actually causes more harm than good.

There are some fractures where it is not appropriate for you to apply an immobilising bandage. These are fractures of the forelimb above the elbow or those of the thigh. This is because it is very difficult to immobilise the shoulder or hip. Bandaging limbs with fractures at these locations will always be detrimental. Similarly applying a bulky, heavy bandage to the limb of a

Do not attempt to place immobilising bandages to fractures of the upper forelimb or thigh.

small dog (less than 10kg) has the potential to weigh down the small limb excessively. In these cases you should take your dog to a veterinarian with no bandaging. You should still try to keep your dog as quiet as possible and the limb as still as possible. Do not attempt to apply an immobilising bandage if your dog is struggling too much as this also has the potential to cause more harm.

Applying immobilising bandages to fractured limbs is similar to applying bandages to skin wounds on the limbs, see pages 50–51. The main difference is that you should use much more roll cotton in the padded layer of the bandage so that it restricts the limb movement and protects the fractured leg. Not using enough cotton wool may cause the bandage to move the fractured bone ends excessively and cause further

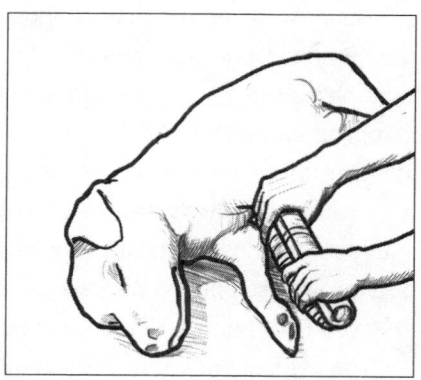

A simple splint supporting broken limb.

damage. If you feel confident you can also fashion a makeshift splint. Possibilities include using a piece of wood or thick cardboard, newspaper or a magazine contoured around the limb. This splint should ideally extend over both joints either side of the fracture. You should attach the splint over the conforming gauze layer using tape around the entire limb at multiple evenly spaced locations. If you do not have tape you can tie it in place using multiple gauze or cloth strips. You can then place the adhesive layer over this.

Spinal injuries

Trauma can cause spinal injury such as a fractured or dislocated back or neck. It can also be caused by a slipped disc. Spinal damage should be suspected after all major trauma. Signs of spinal damage include not being able to move or possibly feel the hind limbs or both the forelimbs and hind limbs. Sometimes the forelimbs may be unnaturally stiff and extended. The dog may dribble urine and may have an unusually open anus. The injured dog may or may not be in a lot of pain. Sometimes dogs with spinal injury are surprisingly comfortable given the degree of their injuries.

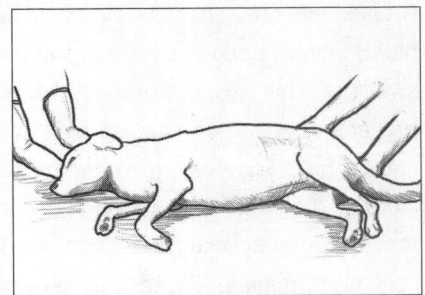
Support dog but minimise movement.

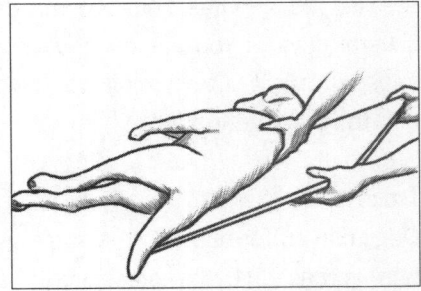
Carefully slide a stiff board under the dog.

If you are at all concerned that a canine trauma victim has suffered spinal injury it is best to play it safe and you should minimise moving them. The safest way to transport them to a veterinarian is to gently slide a stiff board, usually wooden, under the patient. Ideally someone should hold and support the dog during this to minimise movement, especially of their neck and back.

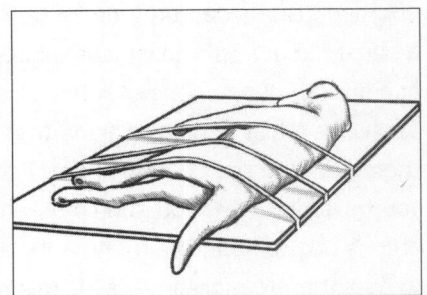
Secure dog with strips of cloth to transport.

You should then use strips of cloth or soft rope tied around the patient and the board to secure them. You can then carefully lift the board and transport the animal to a veterinary hospital.

Bruises

Bruises are an accumulation of blood under the skin or within tissues. This blood initially causes reddening to the skin and their may be some pain and swelling. This blood gradually breaks down changing colour during this process. Bruises can be caused by blunt trauma such as being hit by a cricket ball. They can also occur due to an underlying problem such as a clotting disorder. If your dog has a bruise and you can identify a sensible reason for its appearance, such as mild blunt trauma you can treat this with cool compresses. These can be commercial cool packs or ice or frozen vegetables wrapped in a towel. Cool compresses should be applied to the area for 15 minutes, four times a day until it has resolved. This may take several days. If you are concerned about a bruise and do not know what caused it, or it is becoming worse rather than better, you should take your dog to your veterinarian.

Burns

Dogs can suffer burns in the same way as humans. Often the extent of the burn is masked by the presence of hair over the skin. Burnt skin will be red, swollen and painful. More severe burns will cause the skin to weep, blister and peel. Burns can be thermal due to contact with a hot surface such as a barbecue or a vehicle exhaust pipe, a hot liquid such as boiling water. They can also be due to contact with damaging chemicals. In an emergency situation, the most important thing that you can do for your dog is to remove them from the source of the burn. Again it is vital not to injure yourself. Once you have done this you should aim to minimise the damage caused. If the burn is due to heat, the treatment is copious amounts of cool running water to cool the area for at least 30 minutes.

If the burn is due to contact with an irritant chemical, this should be thoroughly washed off the skin and hair using cool running water and perhaps mild shampoo or detergent if required. You can use a hose to achieve this, however, the water pressure should not be too high as this can be painful. Using multiple buckets of water is also very effective.

Sometimes, if your dog is not being cooperative, using slightly tepid water may help. Once you have cooled the skin or washed off the chemical you should take your dog to you veterinarian. Take the packaging with you. If the burn has been due to a chemical, you should also call the Poisons Information Centre see **Emergency contacts page 111** and see Poisonings on pages 62–63 for further information on irritant chemicals.

You should **never** apply any butter, oils, petroleum jelly or ointments on burns. Instead have them assessed by your veterinarian.

Dogs that have been electrocuted often suffer burns where the electricity as entered their body, often their mouth, and also where it has exited. Once the dog's condition has been stabilised these burns can be treated as described above. Burns in the mouth region may be difficult to cool with water and cool compresses may be more appropriate. Note that dogs that have suffered electrocution may suffer serious consequences such as fluid on the lungs hours after the event and so should be seen by your veterinarian as soon as possible even if they seem well.

> **Regardless of the cause of the burn, it should initially be treated with large amounts of cool running water.**

Self trauma

Sometimes when dogs are very itchy they can lick, chew or scratch themselves excessively. This can be due to many skin conditions including allergies, fleas and mites, contact with irritant substances and acute hypersensitivity or allergic reactions. Licking and chewing generally only causes damage if it continues over a long time. Again you can apply an Elizabethan collar if you have one. You can also try applying a deterrent substance such as Vicks®, Tabasco sauce, or a commercial product like Woundguard® or bitter apple to the area. This will deter some dogs from licking or chewing,

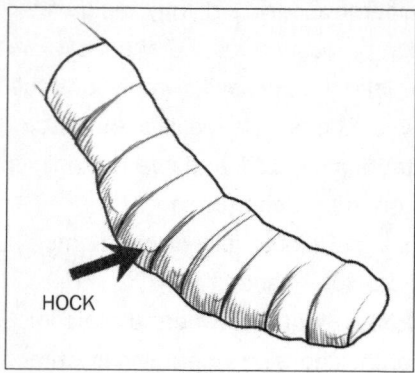

To prevent scratching, first apply cotton roll.

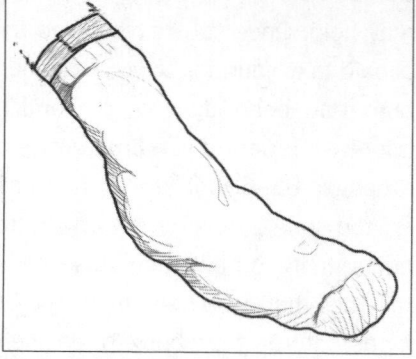

Hind paw covered by a sock.

however most itchy dogs are too determined to be distracted by this. Scratching with the hind limbs can potentially cause serious skin injuries.

If your dog is scratching excessively and you fear that they are damaging themselves you should take them to your veterinarian. Itchy dogs can be quite distressed and you should have the problem investigated and treated as soon as possible. If there is going to be a delay in seeing a veterinarian, you can bandage their hind paws. This covers their nails and helps reduce the damage they can cause. The technique you should use is similar to that used to bandage a limb as described on pages 50–51 but it only needs to cover the paw. First apply a padded layer of roll cotton starting at the toes and covering the whole foot. Continue bandaging upwards to, or just above, the hock. Ensure you have used a reasonable amount of padding over the nails so they are well covered. Apply conforming gauze over this. Finally apply adhesive bandage over this and continue it about 4cm past the other layers so that it sticks to the fur. Alternatively you can use a sock over the paw and attach it to the limb using some adhesive bandage or tape. Some dogs are very good at removing bandages so you may have to reapply them. Putting a deterrent substance such as Vic's®, Tabasco or a commercial product such as Woundguard® or bitter apple on the bandages may help stop them chewing them off.

Nose Bleeds

Dogs can suffer nose bleeds for many reasons. They may be due to a knock or scratch to the nose. They also occur due many other reasons such as high blood pressure, problems with blood clotting, infections and bleeding tumours. You should note if the bleeding is coming from one or both nostrils.

To try to stop the bleeding you can used a cloth to block off the bleeding nostril or nostrils. This may be difficult if your dog is distressed. You can also use a cool pack on the nose to try to slow the bleeding. If the bleeding is profuse or does not stop easily you should take your dog to your veterinarian. If the problem occurs repeatedly or if there is no obvious reason for the bleeding your dog should also be seen by your veterinarian.

Vomiting and Diarrhoea

There are numerous causes of vomiting and diarrhoea. Sometimes the problem can be due to a mild reaction to food or an infection and will spontaneously resolve within several days. Alternatively vomiting can indicate very serious conditions such as pancreatitis, gastrointestinal obstruction, liver, kidney or hormonal disorders or even cancer. Similarly diarrhoea can be due to a mild upset or due to a more serious disturbance. Often it is impossible for you to judge whether the vomiting or diarrhoea is something that will resolve by itself or if it indicates a more serious problem. Recognising Serious Emergencies on page 22 gives some guidelines on whether these problems are likely to be emergencies.

If you feel that the vomiting and or diarrhoea is not, or not yet, an emergency, the the best thing that you can do is to fast your dog for 12-24 hours. Dogs can happily survive a long time without food so this is not at all cruel. When fasting your dog you should never withhold water. If you feel that your dog is continuing to vomit because they are drinking too much at one time, you can give them smaller amounts of water more frequently. Alternatively you can give them an ice block instead of water so that they can slowly drink or lick this as it melts. Young puppies require large amounts of energy and so they should also not be fasted for more than six hours. Similarly diabetic dogs are sensitive to changes in food intake and those that are vomiting or fasted may need to have their insulin dose adjusted, see Diabetes on page 97 for further details.

If the problem seems to have resolved after the period of fasting, you can then reintroduce some bland food. There are some commercial foods that you can obtain from your veterinarian that are suitable for this. Alternatively you can cook some lean boiled chicken and white rice. You should prepare this as around 1/3 chicken and 2/3 rice. Only offer a very small amount initially. If your dog has a good appetite you can then feed small amounts every 6-8 hours for the next day or two. If there are no further problems you can then gradually wean your dog back onto their normal diet over two or three days. All diet changes should be made slowly. If there is any further vomiting or persistent diarrhoea during the fasting, or when food is reintroduced, you should seek veterinary attention. Similarly if your dog is not interested in food after a period of fasting then they should see your veterinarian.

Sometimes a medication your dog is taking can cause vomiting or diarrhoea. Other medications should be stopped if this occurs. Examples are non-steroidal anti inflammatory drugs (NSAIDs). Another example are drugs used to treat Cushing's disease, most commonly Mitotane (Lysodren®). If vomiting occurs during treatment with these drugs you should stop them immediately. Your veterinarian may have given you additional instructions on what to do if this occurs which you should follow. See your veterinarian as soon as possible. Some antibiotics will cause vomiting and diarrhoea and if this occurs you should discuss it with your veterinarian.

Other treatments for vomiting and diarrhoea should only be used if they are specifically prescribed by your veterinarian.

Vomiting can also cause a problem if your dog is on regular oral medication. If your dog is vomiting you cannot be sure that they are receiving their medication. This may be especially dangerous if your dog has a medical problem such as heart condition, epilepsy, encephalitis or Addison's disease. If your dog is vomiting and has a life threatening condition requiring long term oral medication, you should take them to a veterinarian because missing even one dose may be dangerous. Your veterinarian may be able to give the medication or an alternative medication as an injection rather than orally.

Constipation

Constipation can range from mild to very severe and can cause anything from mild discomfort to serious illness. The cause can be dietary, such as eating too many bones, or hair if the dog hunts wild animals. Blockages to the bowel by swallowed objects or tumours can also cause constipation. It can also be caused by disease of the bowel or dehydration.

Constipated dogs will either not produce any feces for a day or longer or will produce only very small amounts of hard feces. They also may strain to defecate without producing anything and may even cry.

If you suspect your dog is mildly constipated you can add ½ tsp of psyllium husk (Metamucil® original) per 10kg of body weight to their food twice a day. If there is no improvement or if your dog becomes unwell or distressed you should take them to your veterinarian. Do not use laxatives, suppositories or enemas designed for humans unless specifically prescribed by your veterinarian.

Poisonings

Substances that are hazardous to dogs can be found throughout the home and often in places dogs visit. The best way to avoid poisoning in your dog is to have all hazardous substances stored safely away from them. Despite all possible care, dogs become exposed to poisons and can become seriously ill. Occasionally poisonings are malicious acts of cruelty to animals.

This chapter will outline some of the more common poisonings in dogs. As far as you are concerned, for the purpose of emergency treatment, poisons can be divided into two major groups. There are those where decontamination procedures, including inducing vomiting, may be beneficial and those where you should not induce vomiting. I describe how you should induce vomiting, and specific situations where you should not, in the sections: Inducing Vomiting on pages 64–65 and Poisonings where you should not induce vomiting on page 76.

There are thousands of substances that could poison your dog, including numerous prescription medications. Not all of them can be listed here. If you are unsure about a particular substance call the Poisons Information Centre (see Emergency contacts page 111 for the number relevant to your country) as well as informing your veterinarian.

If you suspect that your dog has been poisoned it is very important that you keep the packet so that you can discuss the contents with the Poisons Information Centre or a veterinarian. Try to estimate how much of the product that your dog has eaten. You should also take the packet when you take your dog to your veterinarian. Each packet will have a brand name on it, but will also list the active ingredients and the concentration. It may also have some basic first aid instructions. You should take in a sample of your dog's vomit if there is any.

Decontamination

Decontamination involves removing the ingested poison from the body. This can be from an external surface such as the skin or eye, or internally from the gut. This is generally something that is best done by your veterinarian. If the intoxication has only just happened or if there is going to be a significant delay in seeing a veterinarian then it may be appropriate for you to start decontamination. As far as actions you can take for your dog at home are concerned, it is reasonable to flush a poison from their eyes or wash poison off their skin. If the poison has been ingested it may be reasonable to induce vomiting and attempt to bind the toxin by administering activated charcoal to reduce its absorption.

Washing poisons off the skin or coat

If your dog has suffered a poison on its skin then you should wash it off as soon as possible. This is will reduce or prevent damage to the skin and make it less likely to be absorbed through the skin. It also prevents the dog licking it off and ingesting it. Washing is best done with large amounts of running water rather than a bath where the dog sits in the contaminated water. Either shampoo or detergent can be helpful to remove a poison from the skin or coat. Usually detergents work better, especially for more viscous petroleum-based products. Other solvents should not be used as they can irritate the skin. Using warm water may make the dog more cooperative.

Flushing poisons out of the eyes

If the eyes become contaminated they should be flushed out with large amounts of slightly warm water or saline for 10–20 minutes. You should seek veterinary attention as soon as possible. Also call the Poisons Information Centre (Emergency contacts page 111) for specific advice regarding the particular poison involved.

Inducing vomiting

In some poisonings it is safe to induce vomiting. This can help remove some of the toxin from the body. Inducing vomiting is most useful as soon as possible after ingestion of a poison, while it is still in the stomach. Vomiting is likely to be most beneficial up to two hours after ingestion however still may be of some benefit up to four hours after ingestion. In some cases inducing vomiting may be useful even after this time. The safest way for you to induce vomiting is to administer soda crystals. These will break up into a variety of sizes in the packet and you should pick out and administer the ones which seem appropriate for your dog's size. These pieces can be given as if they were tablets. You should give a small dog the equivalent of about ½–1 tablespoon of these, a medium sized dog may require more like 2–3 tablespoons and a larger dog may need up to ¼–½ cup or more. These are generally quite safe and, if they are going to work, will cause vomiting within 10–15 minutes. If your dog has not vomited within this time you can repeat this dose once. If it is still not effective you can try using hydrogen peroxide.

An alternative way to safely induce vomiting is to administer three per cent hydrogen peroxide by mouth. You should give a teaspoon per 5 kg of body weight up to a maximum dose of 10 teaspoons. Once measured, you can draw the hydrogen peroxide into a syringe or a turkey baster and administer it into the mouth. If you have trouble administering this because your dog is resisting too much, you can give this added to yogurt or ice cream if your dog will eat it this way. If your dog does not vomit after 10–15 minutes you can repeat this dose once. If it is still not effective you should take your dog to a veterinarian. Stronger solutions can be diluted to three per cent. For example, you can dilute a 10 per cent solution by adding one part of a 10 per cent solution to two parts water. Once you have induced vomiting by either method, the vomiting generally continues for several minutes and then resolves. Occasionally vomiting will be prolonged and your dog will need to be seen by your veterinarian.

Some people recommend using ipecac syrup to induce vomiting. This however is not particularly effective and there is the risk of causing toxicity. I do not recommend this. Similarly some people recommend administering large amounts of table salt to cause vomiting. If the dog does not vomit, then this method has the potential to cause salt toxicity. Using salt to induce vomiting is also not recommended.

There are several circumstances when it is dangerous to induce vomiting regardless of which toxin has been ingested and you should **not** do so.

Do not induce vomiting:

- If your dog is already vomiting—there is no need to do so.
- If the poison is strongly acidic or caustic, such as those listed under Poisonings where you should not induce vomiting on page 76
- If your dog is overly weak or collapsed because in this condition they may inhale vomit into their lungs, causing serious complications.
- If your dog is convulsing do not induce vomiting. Again they are at risk of breathing in the vomit.
- If your dog has epilepsy, because vomiting can potentially induce a convulsion.
- If your dog has a heart problem, because vomiting can worsen some heart conditions.
- If your dog has a very slow heart rate (less than 50 beats per minute).
- If the packet, the Poisons Information Centre or a veterinarian advise you not to.

Even if inducing vomiting is successful and large amounts of the poison ingested are recovered, it is still vital that you see your veterinarian as dangerous amounts may still be in the stomach or already absorbed.

Activated charcoal

Activated charcoal can be beneficial in binding some toxins in the bowel to help prevent them being absorbed. It is available as tablets and liquid suspensions and should be given at a dose of 1–2 g/kg. This can be a large amount so it is not always practical for you to administer yourself. It is probably best for your veterinarian to administer this if it is necessary. They will generally use more effective forms and methods. However, if there will be a significant delay in seeing a veterinarian, you should try to administer this as some is better than none. It should be given after you have induced vomiting and the vomiting has resolved. If you have not induced vomiting because the poison was ingested too long ago, you can give it as soon as possible after ingestion.

Do not administer activated charcoal to animals that are vomiting or to animals that are convulsing. Activated charcoal should not be given with food as this will bind to it and reduce its effectiveness. Activated charcoal will also bind to other medications and prevent them from being absorbed. Be careful when giving activated charcoal to dogs on regular medication. Burnt toast is not a substitute for activated charcoal and is ineffective.

Poisonings where it may be beneficial to induce vomiting

Insecticides and snail and slug baits

These are usually organophosphates, carbamates or metaldehydes. They usually come as pellets but are also available in granules, liquid and powder forms. Products based on organophosphate or carbamate are often, but not always, dyed blue and are used against a range of insects including flies, cockroaches and termites as well as snails and slugs. Organophosphates and carbamates are also present in some flea, tick and mite products for dogs including collars, shampoos, sprays, spot-ons and rinses. These products typically do not cause a problem when used in accordance with the manufacturers' instructions. They can become a problem if multiple products are used concurrently or if they are used in sick animals. They can also become a problem if they are ingested. Metaldehyde-containing products are usually dyed green and are only for use against snails and slugs. Some products have taste and smell aversives added to discourage pets from eating them. Unfortunately dogs are often still attracted to these products.

Signs of toxicity due to organophosphate or carbamate include vomiting and diarrhoea. This will often have a blue tinge due to the dye added to the product. There will often be excessive salivation, urination, difficulty breathing, muscle tremors, twitching, weakness and, eventually, complete paralysis. Some dogs will become depressed while others will become hyperactive. In extreme cases affected dogs will have convulsions.

Metaldehyde poisoning causes very similar signs, however vomiting and diarrhoea are rare. If these occur they are likely to have a green tinge due to the dye added to the product. The muscle tremors are likely to be much more severe than with organophosphates or carbamates. Initially they will only occur in response to stimuli such as loud noises however they will progress to occur spontaneously. Convulsions are also more likely. Often the muscle twitching and convulsions will cause poisoned dogs to develop heatstroke. To help keep them cool you can put a wet towel over your dog or spray their coat with cool water while you transport them to a veterinarian. You should turn the air conditioning on high in the car if you have it. If your dog is convulsing try to wipe any excess saliva out of their mouth but be very careful to avoid being bitten.

If you suspect that your dog has ingested an insecticide or snail and slug bait or they have a large amount on their skin, take them to a veterinarian as soon as possible. Small dogs and puppies can become severely affected by even just a few pellets. Dogs poisoned by these products can deteriorate quickly. Delaying treatment can worsen their prognosis. Unfortunately, because some of these products can cause a rapid onset of convulsions and fits, it may be unsafe to start decontamination at home. If the ingestion was less than 15 minutes ago and there is going to be a delay in reaching a veterinary hospital, you should start decontamination procedures unless there is a reason not to as outlined in Decontamination on page 63. Do not induce vomiting if the poison was ingested longer than 15 minutes ago. Take your dog directly to a veterinarian instead. If the product was ingested more than 15 minutes ago and you cannot go straight to a veterinary hospital, call the Poisons Information Centre (Emergency contacts page 111) or a veterinarian to check if it is safe to induce vomiting.

Rat and mice baits

Rat and mice baits or rodenticides are very dangerous and are designed to be attractive to rats. This means they are also attractive to dogs. The most common type blocks vitamin K recycling. Vitamin K is vital for the body to make blood clotting factors. As a result this type of bait stops the blood clotting and causes excessive bleeding. These products are extremely potent and eating a rat killed by the toxin is often enough to cause toxicity. Bleeding is not immediate and instead it usually occur from 36–48 hours after ingestion. In some cases symptoms may not be apparent until up to one week after exposure. Internal bleeding may not be obvious. If you suspect that your dog has ingested rodenticide but appears normal, they are still at grave risk and need to see your veterinarian.

If you believe that the ingestion was more than eight hours ago you should take them to your veterinarian to receive the antidote, which is a special form of vitamin K, and any other supportive treatments considered necessary. Because your dog is at risk of bleeding easily you should handle them very gently and keep them calm. Only feed them soft food. Because newer forms of rodenticides are very long acting, a long treatment course is likely to be necessary. If the baits were laid by professionals, you should contact them to find out the exact substance that they used.

Another type of rodenticide is a massive overdose of Vitamin D, which causes blood calcium to rise to toxic levels. Symptoms first appear 12–36 hours after ingestion and include progressive depression, increased thirst and urination and ultimately death. This second type of rodenticide is now quite rare and your dog is only likely to be exposed if it has access to old packets that have been stored.

As your dog may have become poisoned by eating a dead rat or mouse, the poison may have been laid by one of your neighbours. It is vital to discover whether your dog may have been poisoned. From my experience it is important to be as diplomatic as possible when asking your neighbours about this. If you are aggressive and accusatory they are more likely to deny everything. Not having this information may put your dog at risk.

If you suspect that your dog has ingested a rodenticide you should take them to your veterinarian immediately. If there is going to be a delay you should start decontamination procedures unless there is a reason not to as outlined in Decontamination on page 63. Unlike most poisons, rat and mice baits may remain within the stomach for up to eight hours so decontamination even at this late stage may be beneficial.

1080

1080 is a highly regulated poison used in some larger baiting programs. It was originally developed as a rodenticide but is now used to bait foxes, feral pigs, rabbits and wild dogs. It is extremely toxic and ingestion will rapidly kill a dog. Symptoms occur within two hours of ingestion and are initially restlessness, irritability and aimless wandering. They rapidly progress to frenzied running with barking and howling. Convulsions start to occur and become progressively more frequent. The dog may vomit and have diarrhoea with continued straining to defecate and urinate. Over time the poisoned dog will become exhausted, collapse and eventually die. Baited areas are often marked as such and information about baiting programs may be available in local circulars. If you suspect that your dog has ingested 1080 you should taken them to your veterinarian urgently.

Prescription and over-the-counter medications

Below is a list of poisonings in dogs due to common medications available over-the counter and through prescriptions. If your dog has ingested a prescription or over-the-counter medication, you should contact the Poisons Information Centre, see page 111, or a veterinarian to help ascertain whether the dose of that drug is likely to cause a problem in your dog.

Paracetamol

Paracetamol has the potential to be very toxic to dogs and should only be used according to direct instructions from your veterinarian. At excessive doses it has the potential to cause liver injury or failure and changes to the oxygen carrying ability of the blood. It is much easier for small dogs to become intoxicated and even one tablet may be dangerous. Sometimes dogs will ingest large numbers of tablets. You should contact the Poisons Information Centre (Emergency contacts page 111) or a veterinarian to determine whether the dose your dog has received is likely to be harmful. These tablets are designed to be absorbed very quickly.

If there is going to be any delay in taking your dog to your veterinarian then you should start decontamination procedures unless there is a reason not to as outlined in the Decontamination section on page 63. If this is to be effective, decontamination needs to be performed within 1–2 hours of ingestion. All dogs suspected to have accidentally ingested paracetamol should be taken to a veterinarian.

Non-steroidal anti-inflammatory drugs (NSAIDs)

Non-steroidal Anti-inflammatory drugs or NSAIDs are commonly use in both human medicine and veterinary medicine to treat a variety of conditions. Many can be purchased over-the-counter from supermarkets and chemists. As a result they are a common household item. Unfortunately dogs some-times find them and become intoxicated. Sometimes owners also acciden-tally give an overdose of an NSAID that has been prescribed to their dog.

The different NSAIDs vary in their toxicity to dogs. NSAIDs can cause ulcers in the stomach and intestines and bleeding into the gut. In extreme circumstances they can cause perforation of the bowel. They can some-times damage the kidneys and occasionally the liver. The NSAIDs intended for use in humans such as aspirin, ibuprofen, naproxen, indomethacin and diclofenac are generally more toxic to dogs than those specifically designed for use in dogs. So if your dog has ingested one of these, even a very low dose should be considered potentially toxic.

Some NSAIDs registered for use in the dog are in the form of flavoured chewable tablets or flavoured liquid. This means that dogs may be attracted to them and may become intoxicated. It is especially important to keep these medications out of your dog's reach to avoid massive overdoses.

If your dog has been poisoned by ingesting NSAIDs you should take them to your veterinarian as soon as possible. If there is going to be a delay you should start decontamination procedures unless there is a reason not to as outlined in Decontamination on page 63. This should be started within one to two hours of ingestion. Some NSAIDs used in people have a coating which delays their release and means that they may remain in the stomach for longer so decontamination efforts may still be worth while up until four hours after ingestion. If the medicine was obviously ingested more than six hours ago vomiting may actually aggravate any stomach ulcers that may be developing. You should not induce vomiting in this case.

It is usually safe to induce decontamination procedures if you suspect that your dog has ingested another type of prescription medication as long as you follow the guidelines outlined in Decontamination on page 63.

Other Poisons

Nicotine

Dogs sometimes become poisoned by nicotine when they ingest cigarettes or nicotine patches, lozenges or gum. The signs of nicotine toxicity include hyperactivity, vomiting, salivation and progressively worsening tremors. Intoxicated dogs may have difficulty breathing and will become weak and eventually paralysed. Untreated it can result in death. If you suspect that your dog has been poisoned by nicotine you should take them to your veterinarian immediately. If there is going to be a delay you should start decontamination procedures unless there is a reason not to as outlined in Decontamination on page 63.

Lead

Dogs can ingest lead in fishing sinkers, curtain weights, solder, lead lighting, lead shot from from cartridges or birds killed by lead shot and from paint flakes or dust from paint made prior to 1950. Lead poisoning causes a poor appetite, vomiting, abdominal pain, diarrhoea and occasionally constipation.

It also may cause changes in behaviour including hysteria and irritability, apparent blindness, dullness and sometimes fits or convulsions. This toxicity usually comes on slowly with continued exposure to sources such as flakes of lead paint or chewing on lead-lighting. In other instances dogs will swallow lead objects whole. If you have seen your dog ingest a piece if lead you should take them to your veterinarian. If there is going to be a delay in doing this, you can induce vomiting to try to recover the object. This may avert toxicity and the need for surgical removal. This should only be done if the object is not at all sharp and does not have any sharp objects such as fish hooks attached. If the object is not easily recovered you should take your dog to a veterinarian.

Automotive radiator antifreeze/coolant

Radiator additives used to prevent freezing or boiling and corrosion are highly toxic to dogs. They are usually based largely on ethylene glycol but occasionally contain propylene glycol. Dogs apparently enjoy the taste of radiator additive and intoxication is common where they have access to it. Radiator leaks and overflow can cause puddles under cars and act as a possible source, especially for small dogs.

Around 1-4 hours after ingestion, dogs will take on a drunken type state and may drink and urinate excessively. Affected dogs then become depressed and start vomiting around 4-6 hours after ingestion. This depression will progress and can result in coma or death. Dogs that survive this stage are still at risk of developing kidney failure and may stop producing urine.

If you suspect that your dog has ingested automotive radiator additive you should take your dog to your veterinarian immediately. If there is going to be a delay you should start decontamination procedures unless there is a reason not to as outlined in Decontamination on page 63.

Paintballs

The contents of paintballs used in the popular game 'Skirmish' are toxic to dogs when they are ingested. Signs of intoxication include vomiting and diar-rhoea, poor coordination, tremors and, in severe cases, fits or convulsions.

Most signs occur within an hour of ingestion. If you suspect that your dog has ingested paintballs you should take them to your veterinarian immediately. If there is going to be a delay and the paintballs were ingested within the last hour, you should induce vomiting as long as there is no reason not to as outlined in Decontamination on page 63. Activated charcoal is unlikely to be of any benefit.

Fertiliser

Eating fertiliser can cause dogs mild to severe gastrointestinal upsets. Signs of this include a poor appetite, vomiting, diarrhoea and abdominal pain. Your dog may start drinking and urinating more. If the amount that your dog has ingested is very large there is the potential for the blood's ability to carry oxygen to be reduced. If your dog has ingested fertiliser you should take them to your veterinarian. If there is going to be a delay you should start decontamination procedures unless there is a reason not to as outlined in Decontamination on page 63.

Onions and garlic

Onions, garlic and garlic oil can cause toxicity in dogs by damaging the red blood cells and causing anaemia. This is not an acute problem and the dog is not likely to become anaemic or unwell until several days after ingesting the onion or garlic. However, if you suspect that your dog has very recently ingested onions or garlic, you may be able to avert a problem by starting decontamination procedures unless there is a reason not to as outlined in Decontamination on page 63. You should still take your dog to your veterinarian to have them monitored for signs of anaemia.

Grapes

Recently grapes and their products including sultanas, raisins and fermenting crushed grapes have been found to be highly toxic to dogs. Ingesting these products causes kidney failure. Dogs may vomit soon after eating grape products. Intoxicated dogs then stop eating, become depressed, show signs of a painful belly and start passing diarrhoea (often with undigested grapes or raisins). They may produce only small amounts of urine or even none at all. Although toxicity usually occurs when large amounts of these products have been ingested, there are reports of toxicity when only small amounts of sultanas or raisins have been eaten. If your dog has eaten any grape product you should take them to your veterinarian immediately. If there is going to be a delay you should start decontamination procedures unless there is a reason not to as outlined in Decontamination on page 63.

Although only recently recognised, this is a serious toxicity and some dogs do not survive even with prompt treatment. It is not known whether feeding the occasional grape or sultana to your dog as a treat causes long term damage. I do not recommend feeding any grape product to your dog.

Macadamia nuts

Macadamia nuts are poisonous to dogs. They can cause joint pain, especially of the hind limbs, lameness and reluctance to stand or walk. They can also cause weakness, depression and vomiting. Unshelled nuts can cause a bowel obstruction if eaten. If your dog has ingested macadamia nuts you should take them to your veterinarian.

Xylitol - artificial sweetener

Xylitol is an artificial sweetener found in some diet food products. It is toxic to dogs because it causes their body to release too much insulin which dangerously lowers their blood glucose. This causes weakness, collapse and can lead to fits or convulsions, see page 95 and 99.

If your dog has eaten a product containing xylitol you should take them to your veterinarian immediately. If there is going to be a delay and they have eaten the product within 30 minutes and are not showing any signs you can induce vomiting as long as there is no reason not to as described in Decontamination on page 63. Activated charcoal is unlikely to be of any benefit.

Chocolate

Chocolate toxicity is a serious condition which occurs most often around festive periods especially Easter. Chocolate contains several compounds which are poisonous to dogs. Different forms of chocolate contain different amounts of these compounds. Cooking chocolate is the most toxic form followed by dark chocolate. Milk chocolate is moderately toxic and white chocolate is only minimally toxic. Coffee beans also contain a large amount of caffeine which is one of the toxic compounds in chocolate and these too can be toxic.

The amount of chocolate needed to kill a dog depends on the type of chocolate and the size of the dog. For example a 5kg dog such as a chihuahua or maltese terrier can die after eating 250–500g of milk chocolate, 85–180g of dark chocolate or 30–60g of cooking chocolate. Whereas a lethal dose for a 30kg Labrador is 1400–2800g of milk chocolate, 500–1000g of dark chocolate or 180–360g of cooking chocolate. However, signs of toxicity can be seen at doses as low as one tenth of these. Severe signs are seen at doses upwards of one quarter of these.

Signs of toxicity usually occur within two to four hours of ingestion. Affected dogs are initially restless, hyperactive, pant excessively and have a very rapid heart rate (often over 200 beats per minute). They may vomit and occasionally have diarrhoea. Symptoms progress to excessive thirst and urination, muscle tremors and eventually fits or convulsions. Severe toxicity can cause the heart to beat very quickly and irregularly and can result in sudden death. Ingesting large amounts of fat in the chocolate also has the potential to cause vomiting, diarrhoea and even pancreatitis, see page 29.

Chocolate toxicity can be a very serious condition. If you suspect that your dog has ingested chocolate you should take them to your veterinarian as soon as possible. If there is going to be a delay you should start decontamination procedures unless there is a reason not to as outlined in Decontamination on page 63. You should keep your dog very quiet as their heart is at risk of abnormal rhythms for up to two or three days after the ingestion. You should also provide free access to drinking water.

Poisonings where you should not induce vomiting

Poisonings due to some substances are better dealt with by dilution rather than decontamination. This is largely because these substances are direct irritants and vomiting has the potential to cause further damage to the delicate food pipe and mouth. Activated charcoal generally does not bind them effectively. Dilution can be achieved by giving water, milk or egg whites. If your dog does not want to drink or eat any of these you can administer them via a syringe. You should not do this if they are very weak or collapsed as they may inhale anything given orally into their lungs.

Soaps, shampoos and detergents

The degree of toxicity caused by soaps, shampoos and detergents varies markedly from product to product. Most products cause only mild problems while some can cause life-threatening problems. Products containing disinfectants are more likely to be dangerous, as is automatic dishwasher detergent. You should always contact the Poisons Information Centre (see Emergency contacts on page 111) and a veterinarian regarding a specific product. If one of these products is ingested they usually cause nausea, vomiting, diarrhoea and abdominal pain. If you suspect that poisoning has occurred you should start dilution by administering water, milk or egg whites and take your dog to your veterinarian. More serious poisonings also involve muscle twitching, weakness, depression and fits or convulsions. In this case you should **not** start dilution. Instead take your dog directly to a veterinarian.

These types of compounds are unlikely to damage the skin unless there is repeated exposure. However, if they do come into contact with the skin they should always be rinsed off. A mild soap is useful to help ensure that you remove all of it.

Cleaning products

Cleaning products often contain a large range of toxic compounds including pine oil, phenol and turpentine and are more toxic than shampoos and detergents. You should always contact the Poisons Information Centre

(Emergency contacts page 111) and a veterinarian regarding specific products. Poisoning with cleaning products can cause excessive salivation, vomiting, weakness and depression. They can also cause difficulty breathing. They can cause irritation where they have contacted the skin and severe damage to the surface of the eyes. If they are ingested, you should start oral dilution by administering water, milk or egg whites. This should not be done if your dog is very weak or collapsed. If the toxin is on the skin or in the eye you should wash it off thoroughly as described in Decontamination on page 63 and take your dog to your veterinarian.

Corrosives

Corrosive substances are found in many different products including drain cleaners, toilet bowel cleaners, rust remover, metal cleaners and radiator cleaners. You should always contact the Poisons Information Centre (Emergency contacts page 111) and a veterinarian regarding poisoning with a particular product. Ingestion will cause difficulty swallowing, a poor appetite, excessive salivation, diarrhoea and vomiting, often containing blood. Corrosive agents may also cause burns when they contact the skin. If ingestion has occurred you should start dilution by administering water, milk or egg whites and take your dog to your veterinarian immediately. If the poison has contacted the skin or eyes you should thoroughly wash these off as described in Decontamination on page 63 and take your dog to your veterinarian.

Petroleum Distillates

Petroleum distillates are found in petrol used in cars and other engines, solvents, paints, paint thinners and some cleaning agents. These products are unusual because if they are ingested they are very likely to be aspirated into the lungs rather than swallowed. This can cause very serious pneumonia. Signs can occur very rapidly after contact with the substance and include difficulty breathing, coughing, weakness and depression. If you suspect that your dog has been poisoned by a product containing petroleum distillates, take them to your veterinarian immediately.

If petroleum distillates contact the skin they can cause severe irritation and burning. They are also very irritating to the eyes. If contact has occurred with the skin or eyes, you should wash it off thoroughly as described in Decontamination on page 63. You should obviously keep all petroleum distillates and dogs that have been poisoned by them away from naked flames.

Petroleum jelly is not known to be toxic to dogs.

Ticks, Spiders and other Insects

Tick paralysis

Tick paralysis is caused by the paralysis ticks, which occur in bushy coastal areas along the eastern seaboard of Australia from north Queensland to eastern Victoria. Tick paralysis also rarely occur in southern Victoria and Tasmania. They are most prevalent from Spring to Autumn, but can occur at any time of year. Paralysis ticks will jump onto dogs and attach by burrowing their mouth parts into the skin. They can attach anywhere, even in the ears, on the lips or around the anus. However, they usually attach on the front half of the dog. Dogs can have multiple ticks attached at once. Occasionally numerous tiny juvenile ticks can attach and cause a problem.

Once the tick is attached it stays there feeding on the host's blood. During this time the tick also secretes a toxin from their saliva into the dog. This toxin causes the connection between the nerves and the muscles throughout the body to become disrupted, causing weakness and ultimately paralysis. This is not limited to the muscles on the outside of the body but also those inside such as those involved in swallowing in the mouth and the food pipe.

As a very rough guide, for a tick to cause a dog a problem it either has to be quite large (greater than 4mm long) or be attached for at least four days. There can, however be marked variation in the potency of ticks and an individual dog's susceptibility to tick paralysis, which may vary from season to season. Dogs affected by tick paralysis will start to show signs of weakness and become uncoordinated. This usually starts in the hind limbs and gradually progresses forward until the dog collapses. The toxin will affect the voice box so the dog may have a different bark or may not be able to bark at all. This may cause them to grunt when they breathe out. If ticks are attached near the eyes they can make the eyelids paralysed and stop the dog from blinking which can cause their eyes to dry out and become damaged.

Because the tick toxin causes weakness and dilation to the food pipe, affected dogs may retch and regurgitate their food, water or just frothy fluid. One serious complication is aspiration of fluid or food into the lungs, which causes pneumonia. Affected dogs may have difficulty swallowing, which can cause fluid to build up in the mouth and throat choking them. Tick paralysis often causes difficulty breathing. If the paralysis is too advanced, and the muscles involved with breathing too weak, the dog may not be able to breath sufficiently or at all. Tick paralysis is progressive and potentially fatal.

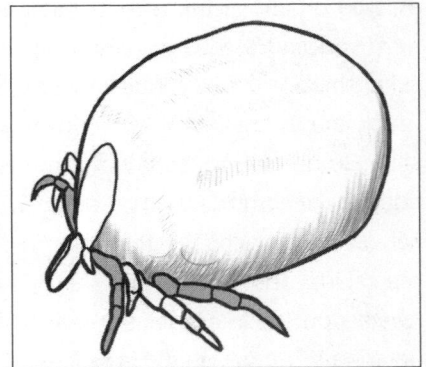

Paralysis tick

Paralysis ticks can be identified by their grey body and the legs around their head. Their legs are the feature which best distinguishes them from other ticks from the same regions, which can also attach to dogs. Unlike other adult ticks, paralysis ticks have one pair of brown legs closest to their head, then two pairs of white legs and one pair of brown legs closest to their body.

If your dog lives in or visits an area where paralysis ticks are present, you should regularly search for them thoroughly. Clipping your dog's coat short, especially during the tick season, makes performing tick searches much easier. To perform a tick search, work your fingers through their coat, down to the skin and systematically massage your fingers over the entire coat. You should concentrate on the dog's front half where they are more likely to occur. Attached ticks are very firmly attached and feel like a hard, smooth round irregularity on the surface of the skin. Make sure you check the edge of the lips, in skin folds and in the ears. If you think that you have found one, part the fur to have a look at it. Nipples, warts and other bumps on the skin are often mistaken for ticks and you should not attempt to remove them. Sometimes the tick has already become detached by the time you perform a search, in which case you may only find a crater where a tick has been attached.

No product absolutely prevents ticks from attaching and causing paralysis so regular searches are vital in avoiding tick paralysis. However, it can be useful to use a product to help prevent tick attachment. These include spot-on type products, baths and rinses and collars.

If you find a tick, you should use a tick remover to detach it from the skin. There are two major types. One is a pair of spring-loaded tweezers which are opened and then closed onto the tick where it attaches to the skin. Be careful not to grasp the body of the tick as this risks squeezing more of the toxin into the skin. The device is then twisted on its axis until the tick detaches. The other type is sickle shaped with a fork in one end. The fork is introduced around where the tick attaches. You then twist the device until the tick breaks free from the skin.

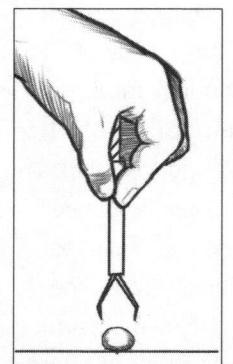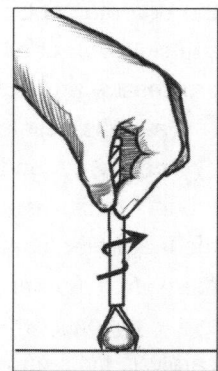

Removing a tick with tweezer-type remover.

Some people suggest applying tick treatments, alcohol, mineral oil or petroleum jelly to the tick. I do not recommend applying anything to the tick before you remove it, nor should you try to burn the tick.

If you do not have a proper tick remover, you can use a pair of tweezers to grasp it at the skin level, being careful not to squeeze on the tick's body. Gently lever it off, rocking back and forward.

If, when you are removing a tick, you leave the head embedded in the skin, a reaction may develop at the site. You should take your dog to a veterinarian for this to be removed.

Once you remove a tick, see if you can identify it as a paralysis tick. If it is a paralysis tick I recommend that you seek veterinary attention. Even once a paralysis tick has been removed it is possible for a do to start showing signs of tick paralysis. Dogs that are showing signs of paralysis can deteriorate further even after the tick has been removed. Many people do not seek veterinary attention after removing a tick from their dog. If you choose not to, put the tick in a well sealed container. If your dog develops a problem it can later be identified by your veterinarian. Many people who have removed ticks from their dog choose not to see a veterinarian when their dog is mildly affected by the toxin, say a little bit wobbly in the hind quarters. In my opinion this is dangerous because of the risk of deterioration. All dogs showing signs of tick paralysis should be seen by a veterinarian and treated. Perhaps I am over

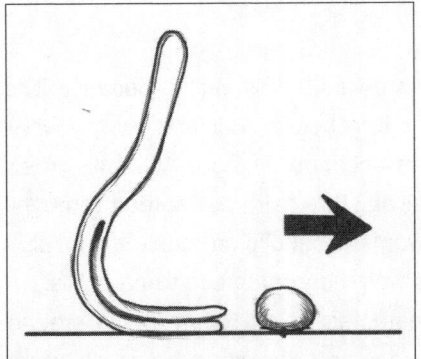 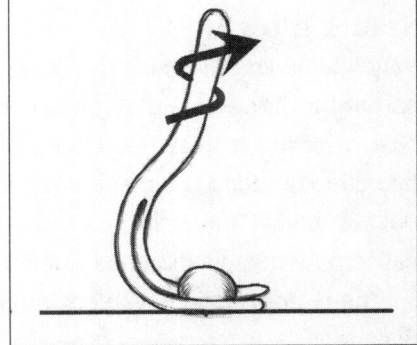

Removing a tick with hook type remover.

cautious and many of these dogs would recover, even without treatment. I just do not think it is worth the risk.

If you suspect that your dog has tick paralysis you can reduce the risk of complications by withholding food and water before you can see a veterinarian. This is especially important if the dog is regurgitating.

Often dogs with tick paralysis become cold or hypothermic. If you suspect your dog has tick paralysis you should take their temperature. If it is below 37.5°C you should start warming them as described in Hypothermia on page 93. Some people believe that dogs with tick paralysis should be kept cold as warming stimulates the toxin. This is false and can actually exacerbate their condition and slow their recovery.

On the way to the veterinary hospital ensure that your dog is breathing well. If they have noisy breathing or are gagging and retching they may have excessive secretions in their mouth. You can try to remove these with your fingers or a cloth, but be careful to avoid being bitten. You can elevate their hind quarters slightly to try and drain these secretions out of their mouth. Lie the dog on their chest rather than side, see page 87. If your dog is badly paralysed and their breathing becomes very weak and shallow, their gums develop a blue tinge or they stop breathing, you will have to start mouth-to-nose breathing as described in Assessing the Canine Emergency Patient on page 35. If their heart stops you may have to perform CPR, see page 43..

Spider bites

Very little is known about spider bites in dogs. This is largely because it is so hard to prove that a dog has been bitten by a spider and exactly what type of spider it was. Red-Back spiders occur throughout Australia. Their bite causes intense pain and often swelling. This pain may spread throughout the body. The venom can cause vomiting and diarrhoea. It can also cause poor coordination and weakness which can progress to paralysis.

The Sydney Funnel-Web spider is restricted to a 160km radius around Sydney. It is a far more aggressive spider and known to be much more deadly to humans than the Red-Back. Very little is known about the effects of Sydney Funnel-Web spider bites in dogs, but they are likely to be less severe than in humans. There are no reports of a bite causing death in a dog. Bites are known to cause short term high blood pressure, rapid heart rates and abnormal heart rhythms in dogs.

If you suspect that your dog has been bitten by a spider you should keep them calm and take them to your veterinarian immediately.

Insect sting or bite allergies

Sometimes when dogs are bitten by insects, most notably bees, they will have an allergic reaction. They may become intensely itchy and agitated or develop hive-type lesions on the skin. Other dogs will develop a character-istic hard, swollen muzzle and possibly puffy, swollen eyelids. The reaction can also make the dog feel generally unwell and they may be more quiet than usual. In extreme circumstances the swelling to the tissue in the mouth and throat can become so great that it impairs breathing. These symptoms can occur immediately after a bite or sting but may take two to four hours to develop. The delay can sometimes be as long as 24–72 hours.

Dogs suffering such an allergic reaction should be seen by a veterinarian. Treatment may be deemed necessary and the dog may also need to be admit-ted for observation for any worsening of the problem. Antihistamine drugs are generally fairly safe and may be beneficial if your dog has an acute allergic reaction. Most antihistamines that you would have at home are not registered for use in dogs and you would be using them at your own risk. You should check with a veterinarian that it is appropriate before giving your dog an anti-histamine. I would only recommend giving your dog an antihistamine at home if the problem is rapidly deteriorating or if you are more than two hours from a veterinary clinic. Below is a table of common antihistamines you may have at home or could easily buy from a pharmacy. The newer antihistamines are marked with an *. These are more expensive but have the advantage of causing less drowsiness. However, less is known about how these newer anti-histamines affect dogs so I recommend using the older types. Avoid using antihistamines in dogs with liver or heart problems, epilepsy or glaucoma.

Name	Formulation	Dose
Polaramine ®		
(dexchlorhenrinamine)	2mg and 6mg tablets	For dogs less than 10kg give 2mg.
	0.4mg/ml elixir	For dogs 10.1-30kg give 4mg.
		For dogs over 30kg give 6mg
		ie. for a 15kg dog two 2mg tablets or 10ml elixir
Phenergan ®		
(promethazine)	10mg and 25mg tablets.	1mg per kg of body weight.
	1mg/ml elixir.	ie a 10kg dog needs
		one 10mg tablet or 10ml of the elixir.
***Telfast** ®		
(fexofenadine)	60mg,120mg and 180mg tablets.	2mg per kg of bodyweight
		Tablet size makes dosing small dogs impossible
***Claratyne** ®		
(ioratadine)	10mg tablets	For dogs less than 20kg give 1/2 tablet.
		for dogs over 20kg give 1 tablet.
***Zyrtec** ®		
(cetirizine)	10mg tablets.	For dogs up to 20kg give 5mg ie 1/2 tablet
	1mg/mL and 10mg/ml elixirs.	or 5ml of 1mg/ml or 0.5ml of 10mg/ml elixir.
		For dogs over 20kg give 10mg
		ie 1 tablet or 1ml of 10mg/ml elixir.

These brands are specific to Australia only and may be replaced by generic antihistamines. Consult your veterinarian for correct and up-to-date information on suitable antihistimines sold in your country. Record their names and dosages in the Notes section on pages 106–109.

You can search your dog's skin for evidence of an embedded insect sting. Often you may not be able to find any sting or obvious cause for the reaction. If you do find a sting, you can try to remove it if you feel comfortable doing so. Do not grasp it with your fingers as this risks injecting more of the toxin into the skin. You can use tweezers at the level of the skin to remove the sting but be careful not to squeeze on the bulb. Instead you could use a stiff piece of cardboard or a credit card by running an edge along the surface of the skin to flick the sting out.

You could also use cool compresses on the swollen areas in an attempt to reduce the swelling on your way to your veterinarian.

Similar reactions can occur after administration of a vaccine or after exposure to certain pollens. Sometimes similar reactions occur when many tiny juvenile ticks are attached to the skin.

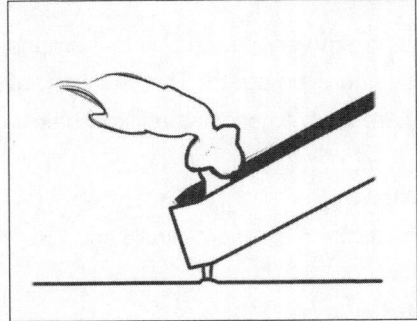
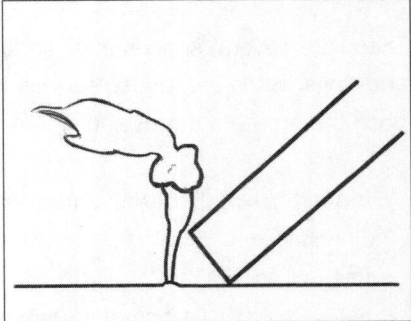

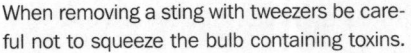
When removing a sting with tweezers be careful not to squeeze the bulb containing toxins.

Removing an insect sting using a credit card.

Anaphylaxis

Just like some people are allergic to certain insect stings, some dogs are extremely sensitive and may suffer anaphylaxis, which is a severe and life-threatening allergic reaction. Dogs suffering anaphylaxis will become weak, may collapse and have signs of shock. For more information about the symptoms of shock see Circulation on page 41. They may appear nauseous or actually vomit. Later they strain to defecate and start passing diarrhoea. In extreme circumstances they may stop breathing or their heart may stop. See Cardiopulmonary Resuscitation (CPR) on page 43 for instructions on resuscitation. If your dog has suffered an episode of anaphylaxis before you may have been dispensed or prescribed an adrenaline injection pen by your veterinarian. If you feel comfortable administering this, do so according to your veterinarian's instructions.

Snake Bites

There are several snakes in Australia which are very dangerous to humans and dogs. Bites can cause serious illness and even death. The snakes that pose the greatest threat and where they are likely to occur are listed below.

Brown Snake: Throughout mainland Australia.

Tiger Snake: South western and south eastern mainland Australia and Tas.

Red Bellied

Black Snake: East coast of mainland Australia.

Death Adder: Throughout mainland Australia except eastern SA and Vic.

Copperheads: South eastern Australia including Tas.

Taipan: Northern coastal Australia including the far north NSW.

Not all snake bites are venomous. However, because venomous snake bites are potentially fatal, all snake bites should be treated as life threatening. If you see a snake near your dog or see your dog attacking a snake and later find your dog collapsed, vomiting, salivating, trembling or inappropriately urinating or defecating, this suggests a potentially fatal bite. Often dogs will seem to recover quickly from this episode but go on to suffer further effects of envenomation. After this initial phase major signs of envenomation that may develop are poor coordination and progressive weakness, eventually resulting in paralysis. Some snake bites have a delayed onset of symptoms, up to several days later. These may include blood in the urine or bleeding due to problems with blood clotting. Sometimes owners will actually see a snake bite their dog. So if you suspect that your dog has been bitten by a snake you should take them to your veterinarian immediately.

Take your dog as quietly as possible, preferably carrying them. Exercise will speed up the spread of venom around the body.

If your dog collapses or becomes limp and paralysed while you transport them, you should keep them lying on their chest rather than on their side. It is easier for them to breathe in this position.

When dogs start to become paralysed by a snake bite, lots of saliva can build up in the mouth and can block their airways. You should elevate their hind quarters, which tends to drain this out of their mouth. You can also use your fingers or a cloth to remove some of it but be careful to avoid being bitten. If, during your trip to the veterinary clinic, your dog's breathing becomes weak and shallow, if their gums develop a blue tinge or if they stop breathing, you will have to start mouth to nose breathing as described in Assessing the Canine Emergency Patient on page 35.

If their heart stops then you may have to perform CPR, as described on page 43. Be gentle when doing this as some snake bites stop the blood from clotting and chest compressions can cause bleeding.

If there is going to be a significant delay in reaching a veterinary clinic, and the bite was on a limb, you can apply a pressure bandage to slow the movement of the toxin from the bite site around the body. This should be applied firmly to help prevent the venom spreading. First apply a layer of cotton roll bandage. This should start higher on the limb than the bite and continue down to the toes. You should then apply a

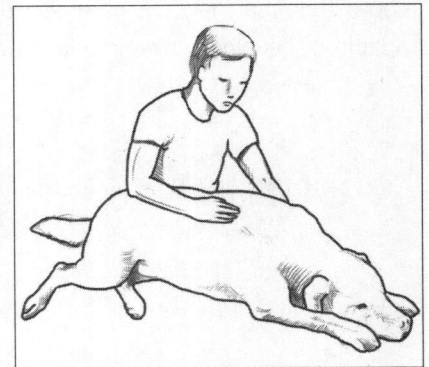

Paralysed dog being supported while lying on its chest

firm layer of conforming gauze over this. You can either stick the bandage on with adhesive tape or apply a layer of adhesive bandage over this. If you are using adhesive bandage, again start above the bite and continue down towards the toes. If you do not have any bandaging material you can fashion a pressure bandage out of clothing. Unfortunately snake bites are often either impossible to find or on the dog's face. If this is the case you should just keep your dog as calm and still as possible while travelling to your veterinarian.

Do not cut into the bite site, attempt to suck out the venom, apply ice to the bite or use a tourniquet on a bitten limb.

It helps the veterinarian treating your dog to know what type of snake caused the bite. If you saw the snake try to describe it as best you can. Unfortunately studies have shown that Australians are generally inaccurate in identifying snakes. Snakes are only correctly identified about 20 per cent of the time. This is probably largely due to the fact that the appearance of each type of snake varies. It is also difficult to accurately identify snakes from a distance. Because of the potential for snakes to be identified incorrectly, I have not included detailed descriptions of each type of snake here. If the snake has been killed, take it to the veterinarian so that they can try to identify it using special keys. They may be able to identify it using a venom detection kit. Be careful with dead snakes as the fangs are still capable of causing envenomation. Only bring the snake in if it is dead.

DO NOT risk being bitten yourself by trying to bring in a live snake.

Heatstroke

Heatstroke is a very serious condition caused by a marked elevation in body temperature. It usually occurs on hot or humid days, especially if a dog has been confined to a hot place such as a car. Dogs can also become overheated after too much exercise and over exertion. Dogs do not sweat significantly. They mainly control their body temperature by increasing their rate of breathing and panting. If a dog's breathing is hindered they can lose control of their temperature and become overheated.

Dogs with shorter noses such as Bulldogs and Pugs are more at risk of suffering heatstroke than dogs with longer noses, which tend to cope with heat better. Puppies, obese dogs and old dogs are at increased risk of heatstroke. Dogs with very thick coats such as Malamutes can easily become overheated. Dogs that have previously had an episode of heatstroke are more likely to have another. As these dogs are very sensitive, special care should be taken not to allow them to overheat.

Dogs rely on their breathing to help keep them cool. If this is compromised it increases the risk of heatstroke. Things that cause problems with breathing are often due to structural problems with the upper airway (the back of the mouth, throat and voice box or larynx). Dogs can either be born with these or they can develop. Dogs with problems in this area will often have very noisy breathing and they may also snore excessively. Problems with the upper airways often occur in dogs with shorter noses including Bulldogs and sometimes Staffordshire Bull Terriers. Older, large breed dogs such as Labrador Retrievers can also suffer laryngeal (voice box) paralysis and have breathing problems. Any dog can potentially have an airway problem. If your dog has been diagnosed with, or you suspect that they have an airway problem, you should take special care to avoid them overheating, especially on hot or humid days. On hot days these dogs will start panting to try to cool down. Because they cannot move air properly they are ineffective panters and continue to heat up and become more agitated. This makes them try to pant harder, exacerbating the problem and leading to a vicious cycle where they can easily overheat.

Dogs kept in cars or confined to other hot areas on hot or humid days risk suffering heatstroke. The risk is increased because they often do not have access to water. Dogs can suffer heatstroke after being confined to a sealed car for only a very short time.

Prolonged convulsions or fits (more than five minutes in duration) or repeated convulsions or fits due to any cause will often cause an elevated body temperature. Heatstroke can be a complication of this, please see Convulsions, fits and seizures on page 95 for further information.

Heatstroke affects the entire body and can cause anything from very mild signs to severe and life-threatening conditions. You should take your dog's temperature rectally as described on page 14. Dogs suffering heatstroke will usually have an elevated body temperature (higher than 39.5°C). Sometimes a dog suffering from heatstroke may have had a chance to cool down and have a normal or only slightly elevated temperature by the time that you measure it. Other symptoms your dog may exhibit include persistent panting, brick red gums, dullness, nausea, vomiting and diarrhoea, an elevated heart rate (faster than 120 beats per minute), weakness and muscle tremors. When it is more severe they may become confused, collapse or have convulsions. The most important way for you to recognise heatstroke is to identify whether your dog is at risk of suffering heatstroke and whether they have an elevated temperature.

Risk factors for heatstroke include:
- Hot or humid day
- Excessive exercise
- Confined to hot area such as a car or shed
- Breed: being a non-athletic, short-nosed breed rather than a more athletic, long-nosed breed.
- Noisy breathing or airway problems
- No access to water
- Prolonged or repeated seizures

Fevers can also cause an elevated temperature and be confused with heatstroke. Fevers are often caused by an infection but can occur with any condition causing inflammation or even with cancer. You should not try to cool a dog with a fever, instead you should take them to a veterinarian immediately. Fevers can occur in the absence of any of the risk factors for heatstroke. The most important way that you can distinguish heatstroke from fever is to identify the risk factors for heatstroke, such as being kept in a closed car or engaging in vigorous exercise on a hot or humid day. Fevers are rarely hotter than 41ºC. You should NOT use medications such as aspirin or paracetamol to treat a dog with either a fever or heatstroke.

If you suspect that your dog has suffered heatstroke and has an elevated temperature then you should try to cool them down and take them to your veterinarian as soon as possible. The best way to achieve both of these goals in a timely fashion is to spray their coat with cool water or cover them with a wet towel and take them to your veterinarian immediately. You should turn your car's air conditioning to maximum or open the windows. Take this approach if your dog is collapsed, convulsing or non-responsive. However, if there is going to be a significant delay in seeing your veterinarian, try to cool them down more aggressively yourself.

Take the dog out of the sun or hot area to a cooler, shaded place and offer them water. Dogs with a temperature of less than 40.5ºC should have a fan placed in front of them. Take their temperature every 15 minutes to make sure it is coming down. If the temperature is 40.5°–41°C, or if the temperature is not coming down you should also wet their coat with cool tap water or apply a wet towel over them while they are in front of a fan. Dogs with a temperature of more than 41°C should be placed in a cool swirling bath. Make sure that their head is above water at all times, especially if they are weak. Take their temperature every 15 minutes. Once it is less than 40°C you can take them out of the bath and place a fan on them. If your dog is collapsed, convulsing or non-responsive you should not put them in a bath. Instead, spray their coat with cool water or cover them with a wet towel and take them to your veterinarian immediately. You should turn your car's air conditioning to maximum or open the windows. You should stop all cooling measures once your dog's temperature has come down to 39°C. If you continue to cool your dog there is a risk that you will make your dog too cold which can cause further damage, see Hypothermia on page 93 for more information. Even once a dog's temperature has returned to normal, there is the possibility for large amounts of damage to have occurred. Heatstroke is a very serious condition that can cause permanent damage and even be fatal. Very serious damage is done if a dog's temperature is elevated above 43°C and these dogs may have a grave prognosis. Often dogs with heatstroke will require treatment for several days to weeks.

All dogs suspected of having heatstroke should be seen by a veterinarian as soon as possible.

Hypothermia

Hypothermia is a reduction in body temperature. It can occur in dogs that are exposed to cold or wet weather, especially when it is also windy. It can occur when dogs fall into cold water. As discussed in heatstroke, hypothermia can occur when you cool an animal with heatstroke too aggressively. Some diseases cause body temperature to drop and the same is true for certain drugs. Small dogs and puppies are more susceptible to hypothermia.

Regardless of the cause, hypothermia is relatively easy to detect. You should measure your dog's temperature rectally as described on page 14. Your dog is cold if their rectal temperature is below 37.5°C. The condition of your dog will vary with how cold they are, how long they have been cold and any disease processes which are causing them to become cold. If they are weak, depressed or collapsed they should see your veterinarian immediately. Hypothermia becomes a much more serious concern below 36°C If your dog's temperature is below this for any reason they should see your veterinarian. You can start rewarming your dog on the way to the veterinary hospital.

If your dog's temperature is between 37° and 37.5°C you probably do not need to do anything to actively warm them. You should take them to a warm place and perhaps cover them with a blanket. If your dog has a coat you can put this on. If their temperature is below 37° you should check them for signs of shock as described on page 41. You should be more aggressive with your warming efforts the colder they are. If your dog is wet you should dry their skin with a warm hair drier. Methods you can use to warm up your dog include wrapping them in blankets or towels and using a 'space' blanket if you have one. Bubble wrap packing material is also a good insulator that you can wrap a cold dog in. You can also warm them with radiant or blow heaters. You can also use surface heating devices such as hot water bottles, electric blankets or electric heat pads. These should not be too hot and you should be able to hold them against your skin without any discomfort. This will be a maximum of 41°C for any of these heating devices. Any heating device should not come into direct contact with your dog's skin as they can cause significant burns. Instead, you should have several layers of blankets or towels between the heat source and your dog's skin. Such surface heating devices may work better if they are placed against areas such as the groin region and possibly the armpits. You should change hot water bottles once they are no longer warm to touch because at this point they will not be effective.

You should recheck your dog's body temperature every 30 minutes to an hour to see if your warming efforts are being effective. If your efforts are not being effective you should see if there is something else that you can do for the dog and consider taking them to your veterinarian. If you are transporting your dog you should have the car's heater on high. Rewarming a cold dog too quickly can sometimes be harmful, your aim should be to raise their temperature by around 1°C per hour. You can stop warming your dog once their temperature has reached 38.0°C. Once you have increased their temperature you should continue to monitor it to check if it drops again.

Because hypothermia may be due an underling illness, you should take your dog to your veterinarian to have this investigated.

Convulsions, Fits or Seizures

Convulsions or fits are usually called seizures by veterinarians. They are relatively common and have many causes. These causes can be due to problems outside the brain such as toxins, low blood glucose or liver problems. They can also be due to a problem within the brain itself such as epilepsy, encephalitis or tumours. Seizures can be generalised and cause unconsciousness, rigid limbs, continuous, violent, limb movements or 'paddling', salivation or frothing at the mouth and possibly urination or defecation. Partial seizures vary greatly but usually involve involuntary movements such as facial twitching or changes in behaviour. Sometimes a seizure may just be an episode of staring into space. Prior to a seizure, a period called the aura, the dog may be anxious and behave abnormally. Similarly once a dog has recovered from a seizure, they may be disoriented and are often very hungry or thirsty. They may even appear blind, behave very strangely and sometimes seem demented. This is called the post-ictal period and can last for hours or days, even after only a short seizure.

Seizures are upsetting for onlookers, especially if it is the first time that you have seen one. If your dog has a seizure for the first time, the cause may not be obvious, or there may be evidence that they have ingested a toxin, in which case you should take them to your veterinarian immediately, see Poisonings on page 62. Seizures may occur due to low blood sugar or hypoglycaemia in diabetic dogs that have had an insulin overdose, see Diabetes on page 97. They can also occur in young puppies that have not eaten regularly enough or have been vomiting. Than can also be caused by the artificial sweetner, Xylitol. If you suspect that the seizure has been caused by low blood sugar you should rub some honey or another sweet substance on the dog's gums, being very careful to avoid being bitten, and take them to your veterinarian immediately.

If they recover from the seizure, offer them something to eat and then take them to your veterinarian. When the cause for the seizure is not obvious you should take your dog to your veterinarian as soon as possible.

Regardless of the cause for the seizure you should move any objects such as furniture away from the dog so that they do not hurt themselves. You should not try to comfort or hold the dog as they are usually unconscious and the movements are involuntary. Similarly, do not try to rouse the dog. A seizure will last as long as it is going to last and talking to, yelling at or shaking the dog will not stop it. You should also not put your hand in their mouth as the dog may bite you involuntarily. Dogs rarely swallow their tongue or even bite it. You can start to comfort the dog once they start to recover.

If your dog has been diagnosed with a seizure disorder such as epilepsy and perhaps is on anticonvulsant medication, a seizure may not be as surprising or upsetting and the cause is usually more obvious. So there may be less urgency to see your veterinarian. However, you should take your dog to a veterinarian if a seizure lasts more than 90 seconds. Seizures typically feel much longer than they actually are so you should time this. Sometimes seizures will be continuous without the dog recovering and this can be very dangerous as it can cause the body to overheat and damage the brain. You should also take your dog to a veterinarian if your dog has more than two seizures in quick succession. If your dog is having a continuous seizure or is having seizures one after another you should try to keep them cool while you transport them to your veterinarian. Spray their coat with cool water or cover them with a wet towel and turn your car's air conditioning onto maximum or open the windows.

It is also very important to make the environment as safe as possible for dogs with a seizure disorder so that they do not injure themselves if they do have a seizure or during the post-ictal period when they are very disoriented. Swimming pools and other bodies of water are especially dangerous as a dog can drown during a seizure. Cliffs and other heights where a dog may fall are also dangerous. These areas should be secured so that a dog with a seizure disorder cannot access them.

You may have medication to give your dog if they have a prolonged seizure at home. This may be a drug such as Valium® (diazepam) that can be administered rectally. In my opinion this is not warranted unless the seizure has been continuing for longer than 90 seconds, however your veterinarian may have given you specific instructions for your dog. You can draw the Valium® up into a syringe. The outside of the syringe can be lubricated with water-based lubricant and gently inserted into the anus. The plunger is then depressed and the contents evacuated into the rectum where it is quickly absorbed. Your veterinarian may also have instructed you to give your dog's regular anticonvulsant medication early, as an additional dose or at an increased dose on days when your dog has had a seizure. This is usually very safe but can cause some sedation and drowsiness. If the additional medication is not controlling the seizures or if you have to continue giving additional medication for 48 hours because of ongoing seizures, your dog should be seen by your veterinarian. You should not try to give any oral medication to your dog while they are having a seizure.

Diabetes

Diabetes mellitus or sugar diabetes is a relatively common condition in dogs which causes numerous health complications including an increased susceptibility to infections. The first sign of diabetes is often an increased thirst and urination. Affected animals may have an increased appetite but lose weight. They may also be lethargic. In advanced stages dogs may develop cataracts in their eyes. Dogs with diabetes are more sensitive to other illnesses and can become very sick quite quickly. This is especially true when the illness causes a poor appetite or vomiting. Diabetic dogs can deteriorate quickly. If they are unwell you should take them to your veterinarian as soon as possible.

Low blood sugar (hypoglycaemia)

Diabetic dogs are usually treated with insulin to lower their blood glucose and help control the disease. One of the most common complications of insulin treatment is low blood sugar or hypoglycaemia. Signs of hypoglycaemia include laziness, weakness, poor coordination, a head tilt, circling, twitching, collapse and possibly convulsions.

Hypoglycaemia can be caused by an excess of insulin. One cause of this is an inadvertent insulin overdose. This is usually either a ten times overdose or a two times overdose. A ten times overdose usually occurs when a person not properly trained with insulin administration has misread the syringe and has drawn up ten times the dose of insulin. Two times insulin overdoses usually occur when two different carers both give the dog its insulin injection. You should make sure that everyone giving the injections knows exactly how to do it. Occasionally an insulin overdose occurs if the wrong syringe is used for the insulin. Always insure that you use the correct syringes. Sometimes weight loss, a poor appetite, a change in diet, another drug being stopped or occasionally, strenuous exercise will reduce a dog's insulin requirement. In these cases even their normal dose may cause a problem.

If your dog shows signs of hypoglycaemia you should feed them a meal. If they seem to recover you should continue to feed them small meals at least every few hours until they are next due for insulin. Your veterinarian may have given you specific advice regarding the insulin dose in this situation. These guidelines may involve using urine test strips which can detect glucose in the urine or using a glucometer to measure the glucose in the blood. When reading urine test strips it is important to follow the instruction on the packet exactly. If you have not been given any specific guidelines on what to do if your dog shows mild signs of hypoglycaemia you should call your veterinarian. If you are unable to contact them and your dog is eating well and is otherwise bright, the safest thing is to skip one dose of insulin and contact your veterinarian as soon as possible to ask for advice regarding starting the insulin again. It is not safe to delay seeking veterinary attention if your diabetic dog is not eating well or is sick.

If your dog collapses or starts having seizures you should rub some honey or another sweet liquid such as corn syrup on their gums. Be careful to avoid being bitten. Do not pour anything into their mouth as they may choke on it. This treatment will usually be effective in one to two minutes. Once they have recovered you should feed them something and then take them to your veterinarian. The meal should ideally be a high protein meal such as dog food or meat but you can give them whatever they will eat. If they do not recover within two minutes rub some more honey or another sugary solution on their gums and take your dog to your veterinarian.

Hypoglycaemia caused by an accidental insulin overdose can be very severe. If you realise that your dog has received an insulin overdose you should feed them a meal and take them to your veterinarian immediately. You should take some honey or another sweet liquid with you in case they collapse or start having seizures on the way.

Ketosis

If your diabetic dog is not eating well or is vomiting and unwell, they are at risk of developing hypoglycaemia. You may have been given some advice on what to do with the insulin dose on days where they are not eating well. If you have to alter the insulin dose for more than 24-36 hours this indicates a more serious problem that needs to be investigated by your veterinarian. Diabetic dogs that are unwell are also at risk of developing, or may already have a condition called ketosis (also known as diabetic ketoacidosis or DKA for short). This condition usually occurs because the dog has another illness in addition to their diabetes. They are especially at risk if they have been receiving less or no insulin because you have been concerned about causing hypoglycaemia due to their poor appetite or vomiting. During

If your diabetic dog has not been eating well for 24–36 hours or if they are vomiting, unwell or depressed, they need to see your veterinarian as soon as possible.

ketosis, fat breaks down and toxic by products build up. This causes the dog to have a distinctive acetone smell to their breath. Some people are especially good at detecting ketotic breath while others find it much harder. Your veterinarian may have given you urine test strips that can detect ketones in the urine. Any ketones in the urine are abnormal. When reading urine test strips it is import to follow the instruction on the packet exactly. Sometimes ketosis develops in diabetic dogs that have not yet been diagnosed as such and are not receiving any treatment. Ketosis is a very serious condition which can make diabetic dogs very unwell and can even be fatal. If you suspect that your dog has ketosis your veterinarian needs to see them as soon as possible.

Whelping

Specific information on breeding dogs and whelping is available from other sources. It is common for the owner of a bitch that is having difficulty whelping to delay taking their bitch to a veterinarian. This can be detrimental to both the pups and the bitch. This chapter provides some guidelines on how to identify when there is likely to be a problem with whelping.

The duration of a dog's pregnancy is 58–71 days from the date of mating. Not all matings will result in a pregnancy and it can be hard to detect if your bitch is pregnant because many bitches will have what is called a pseudopregnancy or false pregnancy following a heat. They may behave like they are pregnant but not be carrying any pups. Pregnancy should be confirmed by your veterinarian. Up to one week before whelping, a bitch may undergo several behavioural changes. She may be more restless and agitated or show signs of nesting, including digging at the floor and tearing material. One to two weeks before the due date for whelping your bitch should have access to an appropriate whelping box. The nesting behaviour usually intensifies up to one day before whelping. There may also be milk secretions from the teats up to one day before whelping. It is generally accepted that a bitch's rectal temperature may drop by up to 1°C, 12 to 24 hours before whelping. Leading up to whelping you should check your bitch's temperature three times a day. These measurements should be made at the same time each day. If you notice a temperature drop the measurement should be compared to the average of the previous week's temperature measurements. If the drop is 0.7°–10°C, whelping may follow in the next 12–24 hours. However, this is not completely reliable and whelping does not always follow. Some veterinarians question the accuracy of this technique. Regardless, if whelping has not occurred 12–24 hours after a temperature drop, you should see your veterinarian to investigate this.

You should definitely take your bitch to a veterinarian if more than 72 days have passed since mating and there are no signs of labour.

The entire whelping process may take up to 24 to even 36 hours. The first stage of labour is usually 6 to 12 hours long. It can, however, continue for up to 24 hours. During this time the bitch has uterine contractions which progressively become more frequent. These are not visible externally. Throughout this stage the bitch will be restless, nervous, exhibit intense nesting behaviour and usually refuse food. Sometimes she may vomit, shiver and pant. A poor appetite and occasional vomiting is not a reason to be concerned unless the vomiting is excessive or the bitch is weak or in pain. If she has not given birth to any puppies after 12 hours of this behaviour you should take her to your veterinarian.

The second stage of labour involves dilation of the cervix and passage of the puppies. Before each puppy arrives clear, fluid may be passed. This is often followed by green, black, red or brown discharge. If there is active straining or strong abdominal contractions, and a puppy is not passed within 30 minutes to an hour, this indicates a problem. Similarly, one or two hours of weak, infrequent straining without producing a puppy may also indicate a problem. Although the time between each puppy can vary, intervals of over two to three hours may indicate a problem. If any of these situations occur, and you feel comfortable doing so, you can put on some examination gloves and with lots of lubrication, gently examine the vulva by parting the labia. If you can see a puppy you can gently try to help it out. Do this by gently pulling on the pup in a slightly downwards direction. Only put traction on the pup when the bitch is contracting. Do not pull on the pup's head or neck, instead gently pull from their body or limbs. If you are having difficulty gripping the pup, and it is half out, using a towel to hold it may help. If either there is no puppy visible or you cannot gently dislodge it within 10 minutes you should take the bitch and the other pups to your veterinarian.

It is not unusual for puppies to come out back feet first or in the so called breach position. This is normal.

If your bitch is ever in pain, weak or collapsed during whelping you should take her to your veterinarian.

The bitch usually licks off the fetal membranes that cover the puppies. This helps stimulate breathing in the pup. Once a puppy has been born, if the bitch has not removed these membranes within one to three minutes you should intervene by laying the puppy on a soft towel and relatively vigorously rubbing it with another towel to remove these membranes. You should use a fresh towel for each pup.

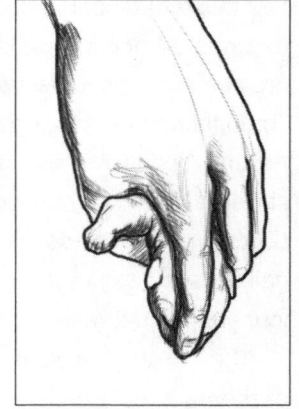

Clearing airways.

If the puppy's mouth and nose is full of fluid you can uses a syringe to gently suck it out or a piece of cloth to wipe it up. If there is a still a lot of fluid, or it is not yet breathing, you can also cup a puppy in your hands with the head at your fingertips and the tail towards your wrist and then gently swing the puppy up and down as if you were chopping wood. You should of course be careful not to let go of the puppy or jar it. If your hands are big enough, you can hold the puppy's body in one hand and use your index finger over the puppy's head to stop it leaving your hand. You can then swing the puppy by gently lifting them up and swinging them downwards four or five times. This helps to remove fluid from the airways and stimulate breathing.

If a pup is still not breathing, continue to rub it for another minute to try to stimulate its breathing. If the puppy is still not breathing after this you should give it five tiny breaths through its nose while holding its mouth shut. Be careful that the breaths are not too big or forceful as you could damage their tiny lungs. You should check if it has a heartbeat by feeling its chest. If it does not have a heartbeat, you should start very gentle CPR as discussed on page 34.

Do not give up easily as occasionally it may take one to two hours for a pup to start breathing for itself. Remember, however, that you also have to look after the bitch and the other puppies.

The bitch usually breaks the umbilical cord with her teeth. If she does not do this you will have to tie it off and cut it. You should use some fine thread to tie a tight knot around the umbilical cord about 3cm away from

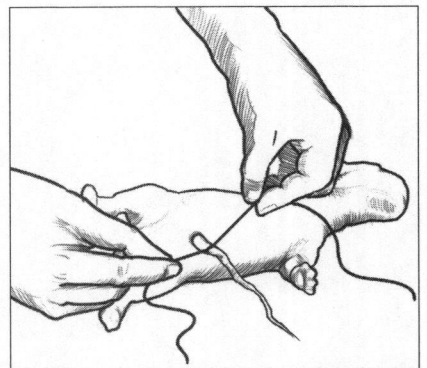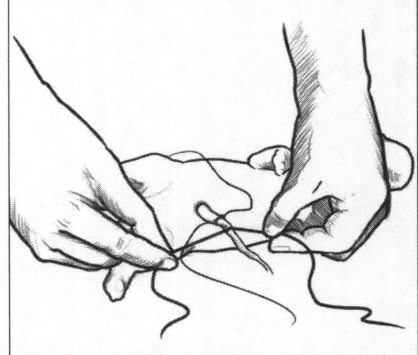

Tying off the umbilical cord of a newly born pup. cut between the two knots.

the puppy's belly. Place a second knot 2cm further away from this and cut between these two knots. Dip the severed ends of the umbilical cord in some Betadine® (povidone iodine solution 10% v/w). Be careful not to pull on the umbilical cord as this can cause a hernia.

Not every puppy will be followed by a placenta and sometimes two puppies will be passed before either of their placentas is passed. It is useful to try to ensure that as many placentas as puppies have been passed. This can be difficult because it is natural for the bitch to eat the placentas. If this is the case do not worry too much about accounting for all the placentas.

Green, black, red or brown vulval discharge in the absence of other signs of labour can indicate a problem and is another reason to take your bitch to your veterinarian.

Index

Emergency Contacts

Australia
EMERGENCY—Police, Fire, Ambulance :.............................000
Poisons Information Centre: 131126
Local Council Ranger phone:.............. After-hours: ....

United Kingdom
EMERGENCY—Police, Fire, Ambulance: 999
For Poisons Information contact the RSPCA
RSPCA 24-hour: 0870 555 5999
Council Animal welfare phone: .... After-hours: ....

New Zealand
EMERGENCY—Police, Fire, Ambulance: 111
National Poison Centre: 0800 764 766
Royal NZ SPCA: 09 827 6094
Local Council Ranger phone:.............. After-hours: ....

Veterinary clinic name:....................................
Veterinarian's name: ....
Phone: .... Opening hours: ....
Address: ....
....

Emergency Veterinary clinic 1 ....
Phone: .... Opening hours: ....
Address: ....
....

Emergency Veterinary clinic 2 ....
Phone: .... Opening hours: ....
Address: ....
....

Your Dog's Health History:

**Vaccinations, Intestinal Worming,
Heart Worm Tests and Prevention, Flea Control, etc.**

Date: . . . .   Comments:. . . . .

Date: . . . .   Comments:. . . . .

Date: . . . .   Comments:. . . . .

Date: . . . .   Comments:. . . . .

Date: . . . .   Comments:. . . . .

Date: . . . .   Comments:. . . . .

Date: . . . .   Comments:. . . . .

Date: . . . .   Comments:. . . . .

Date: . . . .   Comments:. . . . .

Date: . . . .   Comments:. . . . .

Date: . . . .   Comments:. . . . .

Date: . . . .   Comments:. . . . .

Date: . . . .   Comments:. . . . .

Date: . . . .   Comments:. . . . .

Date: . . . .   Comments:. . . . .

Date: . . . .   Comments:. . . . .

Date: . . . .   Comments:. . . . .

Date: . . . .   Comments:. . . . .

Date: . . . .   Comments:. . . . .

Date: . . . .   Comments:. . . . .

Date: . . . .   Comments:. . . . .

Date: . . . .   Comments:. . . . .

Date: . . . .   Comments:. . . . .

Date: . . . .   Comments:. . . . .

Date: . . . .   Comments:. . . . .

Date: . . . .   Comments:. . . . .